Sorority Guide

Everything you need to know from ALPHA to ZETA!

Ceil Howle & Anna Stephens
with Jennifer Brett

Grand View, Inc.
Publisher

Published by
Grand View, Inc.
Atlanta, Georgia

Library of Congress Control Number: 2006926039

Howle, Ceil.
Sorority Guide: Everything you need to know from Alpha to Zeta/Ceil Howle,
Anna Stephens and Jennifer Brett—1st ed.

Summary. Everything you need to know about sororities—resumes,
recommendations, registration and recruitment Advice from experts,
timelines, samples and templates for Greek life. Includes index.

ISBN: 0-9779153-0-1

1. Teenage girls—Life skills guides. 2 Greek letter societies—United States.
3. Women college students—social aspects. 4. Teenage girls—Conduct of life.
5. Initiations.

Printed in the United States of America 1. Title

First printing—May 2006

Edited by Phyllis Mueller
Cover design by Peggy Schultz
Page design by Bonnie Supplee
Original artwork by Holley Henderson

This book is available at quantity discounts for bulk purchase and fund raising
opportunities. For information see www.sororityguide.com

Why You Need Sorority Guide

She got to college with the cutest clothes, the friendliest smile, and the biggest hopes for joining a sorority. But when recruitment ended, she sat stunned as her friends all dashed off to their new houses and she was left without a bid. She was a good student all throughout high school. She was involved in sports, clubs, and several civic groups. She felt like she gave rush her all.

So what happened? Simple. She just wasn't as prepared as the hundreds of other young women competing for limited spots in the sororities on her campus. What she lacked, it turns out, was the right information, at the right time, about preparing for recruitment, what to expect every step along the way, inside tips on what to do, and crucial pitfalls to avoid.

Sorority Guide covers it all—everything you need to know, from Alpha to Zeta. We're here to make sure you arrive as prepared as you can be for recruitment.

We take you behind the scenes as rush begins. We've talked to people from California to Florida, Boston to Austin and back again to let you in on current and alumnae sorority members' top tips for success. And we tell you what they warn a prospective member *never* to do or say.

Sorority Guide has all this and more. We're here to make sure you arrive as prepared as you can. You'll have all the information you need, when you need it, while there is still time to use it.

Even before you know what college you're going to attend, getting the inside scoop on Greek life can't hurt. Your college's Web site will be a great resource for the basics of recruitment – when to register, times, dates, and so on. But *Sorority Guide* has information you won't find anywhere else—a plan and success strategies that could make all the difference.

Let's get started! There are tons of ways to use *Sorority Guide*. Read it front to back or back to front. Have fun with the quiz. Check out our success strategies, or become a sorority fashionista. *Sorority Guide* is full of facts, figures and fun!

Why We Wrote This Book

We were excited when a friend said her daughter planned to register for sorority recruitment. Then she whipped out a flimsy pamphlet about the size of a church bulletin.

"Here's the information she got in the mail," our friend said.

The 4-1-1 was more like no-1-1. No info on what to wear. No rush schedule. No real help at all! Just a few nice words about how sorority life will be such fun.

Well, we thought, this girl needs our help. We thought you might, too.

It's important to pay attention to materials your school mails to you or info you find on the Web—but don't depend on mailers or Web sites to get you ready for sorority life. By the time you register for recruitment, the opportunity to become truly prepared has passed. You must start early to ensure you're a well-rounded candidate, ready to compete.

Depend on us. We're sorority alumnae who went through rush when it was still simple—when girls beat a path to their mother's or sister's sorority house, had some tea, and signed their bid cards. But booming freshmen enrollment means recruitment is more complex and more competitive. Legacy status is no guarantee. At the same time, the benefits of sorority life are increasingly important and extend well past college years. Today's sorority sisters are tomorrow's business contacts.

Sorority Guide will show you some of the benefits of sorority life and help you decide if Greek life might be right for you. Our success strategies will help you get your paperwork and yourself together as you prepare to rush. We'll lead you through the process of finding your best match on campus.

We'll take you round by round through rush, give you a look at recruitment from both sides, and give you a history lesson on sororities. There's info for parents, too, and we'll talk about all the fun you'll have along the way.

Take that church bulletin-sized pamphlet and fan yourself this Sunday. For success strategies, turn to *Sorority Guide*.

All the best, C.H. and A.S.

Table of Contents

CHAPTER ONE

What Is a Sorority, and Why Should I Go Greek?

What Is a Sorority, and Why Should I Go Greek?

You're going to college! This is an amazing time in your life: a time to learn, grow, meet new people, work hard, and have fun—all in preparation for your future. For many of you, this is your first time to be living away from home, and your first time to be surrounded by new faces. Should sorority life be part of your college experience? We want to help you decide and help you get ready!

Sororities are private organizations where members enjoy fun and fellowship, and where they participate in incredible social events and worthwhile charity work. Membership is by invitation, or bid, following a period of recruitment historically known as rush.

Sororities typically are located in houses on or near your college campus, or they may have designated areas called chapter rooms in certain buildings—usually dorms or the student center. The house or chapter room is where you participate in recruitment events, and it's where you later will attend chapter meetings and some social functions. Sorority members who support a house will eat meals there and may live there.

Sororities have been around since the late 1800s. Like fraternities, which are similar organizations for guys, sororities use Greek letters in their names. Many sororities, in fact, are officially called "fraternal organizations for women" or "fraternities for women."

Membership is a big commitment, and there are costs involved. We like to say membership isn't free, but the experience is priceless. As a member you are going to meet girls who will become lifelong friends and potential business associates. You could meet a great guy at one of the many social functions, including sorority-fraternity mixers, where one sorority and one fraternity get together for a theme party or other fun event. Later, you'll enjoy dressing up for formals. Along the way you'll learn leadership and organizational skills, and you'll have the comfort of knowing you've got a place in a relatively small but active group on campus.

Whether the college you've chosen is big or small, for you it's new, and it might even be scary. A sorority can help turns this huge mass of people into a manageable group where you can more easily find your place. If college is a big ocean, sorority life can help you find your current.

The first step in your sorority experience is one you must take alone. You need to sit down and really think about what you want out of your college experience and if you want Greek life to play a part. Sisterhood is for a lifetime, and you need to make sure you're down with that.

While you're getting your thoughts together consider these four Ss of sorority life: **sisterhood scholarship, social life, and service.**

1. **Sisterhood.** You're going to hear this word a lot. Sisterhood means something different to each member. It describes so much, from hilarious memories to special moments you will share with the girls whose Greek family you will join. Years after you have graduated, you and your sorority sisters will share a bond that lasts forever.

2. **Scholarship.** Sorority members do not let each other slack off when it comes to grades. There's a minimum GPA to join, and you've got to keep your grades up once you're in. Studies show Greek women consistently have higher GPAs than non-Greeks. Many sororities offer academic scholarships to outstanding members. Your sorority can help you succeed academically, with tutoring programs, study hours, even with copies of old tests and exams.

3. Social life. Sorority members have a ton of fun! You'll enjoy social events like Greek Week, Christmas formals, scholarship banquets, spring break trips, tailgating before games, and sisterhood retreats. There will be special events for homecoming, pledge formals for brand new members still looking forward to initiation, sports-related events like golf tournaments or Greek Week competitions (a mini-Olympics that raises money for charity), and mother-daughter teas and luncheons. You'll enjoy semi-formals with themes like "Cinderella's Ball" and crush parties with fraternities. The social highlight of the year is often the formal, which might be an elaborate, elegant affair at a resort or hotel out of town

4. Service. Along with socializing and studying, you're going to do some serious good. The National Panhellenic Conference Web site reports over 300,000 service hours and more than $5.2 million are donated by college sororities nationwide each year. Sororities collectively raise hundreds of thousands of dollars for worthy causes like medical research and children's hospitals. Giving of your time and talents can be one of the best feelings you'll ever have. All that volunteering will help develop your talents and will look great on your resume.

Why Go Greek?

Some current and alumnae members we talked to said...

"It gets you ready for just about anything: talking to people you don't know, working with a group, organizing events, and taking leadership roles."

"It helps you keep your grades up. Sororities generally have minimum GPA requirements and often have friendly competition with others to see which house has the highest average GPA."

"It helps you organize your time and be a better multi-tasker. As a sorority member, your schedule will be jam-packed with classes and academic requirements, chapter meetings, dinners at the house, social events, and volunteering. You'll learn to fit a lot into every day."

"Sorority life gets your wardrobe in shape. You'll assemble cocktail and formal outfits for special functions. Chapter and pledge meetings will likely call for nice outfits that will serve you well in your future."

"It may help you choose a career path, if you're undecided. Organizing an event that benefits a children's charity could help you realize you'd love to work with kids, or that you're great at communications. You'll develop skills that will help you professionally after college."

"Sorority members get involved with great causes, like raising money for children's hospitals, cancer research, and other charities."

"Sorority members have more opportunities to get involved in intramural sports including softball, tennis and lacrosse. If you aren't going out for the varsity team but still want to remain involved in your favorite sport, this is a great way to do that."

"You and your sisters will be busy learning about your sorority and participating in fun service and sports-oriented events. All this togetherness will lead to friendships and memories that will last a lifetime."

"Some girls find the guy of their dreams at mixers or other events! Pledge swaps and theme parties are great ways to meet a bunch of great guys."

"It's a quick way to meet a lot of people and have many fun social events to attend."

BOTTOM LINE:

Sororities are all about sisterhood, scholarship, social life, and service. Now that you know a little about sororities, are you ready to find out if Greek life could be for you?

Take our quiz!

CHAPTER TWO

The Sorority Guide Quiz

The Sorority Guide Quiz

Is sisterhood your thing? Our quiz will help you decide.
Answer truthfully and tally your score at the end.

1. When filling out the "extracurricular activities" section on your college applications, you:

   A. Listed a few sports teams and your church youth group.
   B. Considered listing text messaging.
   C. Attached a .pdf file to list all of your incredible deeds.

2. You win a magazine contest, and the prize is an awesome party with a celebrity guest. You invite:

   A. The hottest runway model.
   B. A chart-topping pop star.
   C. Your favorite actor.

3. The most-played bands in your iPod are:

   A. Pop or hip-hop.
   B. Alternative rock.
   C. Country.

4. In class:

   A. You speak up when you have a point to make and really listen when others give their opinions.
   B. You alternate between cracking up with your friends and making subtle eye contact with your crush.
   C. You're pretty quiet and concentrate on work.

5. If you were a circus performer, you would be:

   A. A lion tamer or a trapeze artist.
   B. A clown or a juggler.
   C. The ringmaster.

6. After school:

A. You head straight to the mall with friends, then decide whether you'll try on every pair of shoes in your size or get your manicure touched up.
B. Your day has practically just begun. You're off to a club meeting, team practice, or other after-school event.
C. You go straight home to start your homework or head for your after-school job.

7. At parties, you:

A. Hang out with your close friends.
B. Wear your lowest low-rise jeans with the cutest top you own and make sure everyone checks you out.
C. Spend most of the time dancing.

8. Your favorite saying is:

A. LOL.
B. That's hot!
C. Shut UP.

9. A new coffee shop has just opened. You:

A. Get a group of friends together and make it your regular hangout.
B. Claim a comfy chair where you can sip lattes and log on to the shop's Wi-Fi access to email friends or research papers.
C. Immediately develop a crush on the guy who's home from college and working the counter during summer vacation.

10. Your summer dream job would be:

A. Modeling for the new Abercrombie catalog.
B. Working as a camp counselor or lifeguard.
C. Baby-sitting for a really great family in your neighborhood.

11. Your bling of choice is:

A. Funky, brightly colored earrings.

B. A tiara.

C. A heart pendant.

12. Parties are:

A. A chance to meet new people.

B. A chance to hang with close friends.

C. An opportunity for everyone to admire your new designer outfit.

13. A big exam is coming up. You:

A. Cram the night before, say a prayer on your way into class, and hope lightning will strike and knock out the electricity during the test.

B. Stroll into class knowing you studied faithfully for weeks and completed all homework assignments until you mastered the subject.

C. Wish you had done just a little more to get ready.

14. You exercise by:

A. Racing to the mall to find the latest Kate Spade bag.

B. Working out at the gym with your headphones on.

C. Playing volleyball, tennis, or another team sport.

15. The honor society at your school requires members to fulfill a certain number of hours volunteering for charity. You choose:

A. Habitat for Humanity.

B. The Red Cross.

C. The Humane Society.

16. If you were new in town and wanted to meet a bunch of cool girls in a hurry, you would:

A. Sign up for Pilates at the gym.

B. Look into the youth program at a house of worship.

C. Get a job at the hottest store in the mall.

17. The worst thing someone could do is:

A. Smoke.

B. Steal someone's boyfriend.

C. Talk bad about people behind their backs.

18. When your mother asks, "Are you really going to wear that?"

A. You say, "Yeah!"

B. You ask, "What's wrong with it?"

C. You go back to your room and change.

19. Your proudest moment was:

A. Being crowned homecoming queen.

B. Crossing the finish line at a 5K to raise money for cancer research.

C. Being accepted into the honors program.

20. Your family adopts a puppy from the animal shelter. You name it:

A. Princess.

B. Killer.

C. Lucky.

21. By the time you are 30, you will have:

A. Two cute kids and a hot husband.

B. Your own clothing and perfume line.

C. An Olympic gold medal.

22. Your best trait is your:

A. Loyalty to your friends.

B. Incredible sense of style.

C. Hilarious sense of humor.

23. You look for a guy who:

A. Goes to church and is sweet to his mother.

B. Captains a varsity team.

C. Plays the guitar.

24. When your teacher announces a mandatory project or your coach announces a mandatory practice, you:

A. Immediately log the info into your cell phone's organizer.

B. Break out in hives at the word "mandatory."

C. Roll your eyes but follow instructions.

25. During your high school's Spirit Week you:

A. Ask your friends what they're wearing, then do the same.

B. Get your mother to write you a sick note.

C. Stay up all night making an amazing costume you know no one else will have.

The SG Quiz: What's Up With Your Score?

Add up your score by assigning the following points for each answer:

1. A. 3 B. 1 C. 5	10. A. 5 B. 3 C. 1	19. A. 5 B. 3 C. 1
2. A. 5 B. 3 C. 1	11. A. 3 B. 5 C. 1	20. A. 1 B. 3 C. 5
3. A. 5 B. 1 C. 3	12. A. 3 B. 1 C. 5	21. A. 3 B. 3 C. 3
4. A. 3 B. 5 C. 1	13. A. 1 B. 5 C. 3	22. A. 3 B. 5 C. 3
5. A. 3 B. 1 C. 5	14. A. 5 B. 1 C. 3	23. A. 1 B. 5 C. 3
6. A. 5 B. 3 C. 1	15. A. 5 B. 5 C. 5	24. A. 5 B. 3 C. 1
7. A. 3 B. 5 C. 1	16. A. 3 B. 1 C. 5	25. A. 1 B. 3 C. 5
8. A. 1 B. 5 C. 3	17. A. 5 B. 5 C. 5	
9. A. 3 B. 1 C. 5	18. A. 5 B. 3 C. 1	

How do you rate? Add it up and check yourself out!

If your score was:

25– 50: You're really into your friends. People close to you say you're a special girl, and they know you care. But you're all about the familiar. You're so afraid you'll say the wrong thing that you avoid talking to people you don't know. Sorority life can break you out of your shell and help you chill with new friends. It can help shrink the size of your campus and help you find a group that you connect with.

SUCCESS STRATEGY To overcome shyness during conversations with new people, ask others about themselves. Having an idea of what you'll talk about may help you feel more comfortable. Look for the sample questions in Chapter 4 or on www.sororityguide. com for suggestions. Have three questions ready.

51–70: People say you're quiet at first, but once they get to know you, you're hilarious! You're not the most outgoing person in the world, but developing close relationships with friends is important to you. Sorority life will help you feel less stressed when you're meeting new people and can help you gain the confidence to seek leadership positions during your Greek experience and afterward.

SUCCESS STRATEGY Not every sorority member will be a chatterbox. Helping to carry the conversation with someone more shy than you will make you feel more at ease and help you shine.

71–89: You're into meeting new people, and you're not shy at all. People tell you you're the first girl they met when they were new to school. You don't have to be in the spotlight, though. With your laid-back personality you're sure to find a good fit. You have lots of friends, and probably know many of the other girls going through rush. Remember to be selective, though, and find the best match for you. Don't feel pressured to choose a sorority because your friends seem to like it. You'll make lots of friends no matter where you end up.

SUCCESS STRATEGY Remember that during the recruitment process you're there to choose, not just to be chosen. Challenge yourself to find two or three sororities where you can be yourself.

90–125: You are so into recruitment. You have eight outfits picked out for rush week, and it's only four rounds. You're a triple legacy, and you have five recs for each sorority on your campus. In short, you have no doubt whatsoever you'll get a bid, and you know Greek life is for you. Don't get cocky! It's important to remember that with increasing enrollment, not every legacy is guaranteed her first choice. This is not your mother's sorority experience—make sure you choose what's right for you today. Also keep in mind that Greek life is about teamwork.

SUCCESS STRATEGY If you aren't given a bid to your first choice, that's no excuse for drama. Remind yourself that you stuck it out and got one of your top choices. Bring on the first social!

BOTTOM LINE:

There's no one ideal "sorority type." Greek life will introduce you to a group of girls who come from different backgrounds and have different interests. They could become your lifelong friends.

CHAPTER THREE

Learning the Lingo:

A Glossary of Common Greek Terms

Learning the Lingo: A Glossary of Common Greek Terms

Active: A sorority member who has pledged and been formally initiated.

Advisor: An alumna sorority member who lends her guidance and experience to the chapter.

Advisory board: Sorority alumnae who lend guidance to a chapter of their sorority.

Affiliate: To join a sorority after switching colleges. For example, an XY member at College A who transfers to College B may affiliate with the XY chapter at College B without having to go through any review process.

Alumna: A sorority member who has graduated from college. Active involvement in alumnae chapters is a great way to continue supporting the sorority, maintain friendships, and meet potential business contacts.

Alumnae Panhellenic Association: A group for sorority members who have graduated.

Badge: A pin that initiated members may wear to display their affiliation with a sorority.

Bid: A formal invitation to become a member of a sorority.

Bid Day: The day following the recruitment process that bids are distributed. (This will be a happy day full of joy and relief!)

Big Sister: An active who pairs up with a new member, serving as an advisor, mentor, and friend. The new member she is paired with is her *Little Sister*.

Blackballing: When a potential new member is kept from joining by one sorority member for any reason.

Candlelight: A special sorority ceremony where a sister announces she has become engaged or that her boyfriend has given her his fraternity pin or lavaliere.

Chapter: A local unit of a national sorority on a particular campus, recognized and chartered by the national headquarters of the sorority.

Chapter meeting: A regular meeting, usually held weekly, to discuss sorority business. It is held in the sorority's house or chapter room.

Charter: Permission from the sorority's national headquarters to establish a chapter of that sorority on campus.

Colony: A newly formed Greek letter group awaiting official installation from national sorority headquarters.

College Panhellenic Association: The local group that oversees sorority chapters on a campus.

Colors: The official color or colors of a sorority. Sorority colors often have special meaning.

Continuous open bidding: When a sorority has slots open after formal recruitment and fills them in an informal process.

Crest: A design with special significance, unique to each sorority and fraternity.

Cut: The choice not to invite a potential new member back to the next recruitment party, or the choice by the potential new member not to select a sorority for further visits.

Depledging: When someone who has been given a bid chooses or is asked to leave during the sorority pledge period. She may not pledge a different sorority for a year.

Deferred recruitment/rush: A recruitment/rush process that takes place after formal recruitment/rush.

Dirty rush: When sorority members try to influence girls prior to recruitment by promising bids or otherwise suggesting favorable consideration.

Dropping out of recruitment: Withdrawing from the recruitment process. A potential member should discuss this with her recruitment counselor to ensure proper handling. A potential member who drops out must wait until the next formal recruitment period to go through the process again.

Dry rush: Recruitment where no alcohol is served. Sororities ban alcohol at official rush events during recruitment.

Dues: The ongoing cost of sorority membership. Dues cover the costs of operating the house, social events, and other responsibilities.

Expansion: The process of opening a new chapter of a sorority at a campus where that sorority does not have a presence.

Founders Day: Celebrations honoring the women who founded a sorority.

Formal: A dressy social event that takes place in an elegant setting such as a hotel ballroom or resort, often out of town. Sorority members are responsible for accommodations and meals for their dates during formals.

Fraternity: A Greek-letter social society. Fraternities for women are often called *sororities*.

Greeks: Sorority and fraternity members.

Greek Week: A fun schedule of events involving all Greek organizations on campus to benefit great charitable causes.

Handshake: A special secret greeting unique to each fraternity and sorority.

Hazing: Any inappropriate action that makes a member feel humiliated or that puts them in physical danger. This practice is forbidden, and any incidents should be reported. Schools typically have anonymous tip lines or other means of reporting hazing. Contact your college's office of student affairs for information on reporting hazing.

Hotboxing: Also forbidden, this term refers to the practice of improperly pressuring a potential member to accept a bid.

House: The physical building where a sorority is located.

In-house: A sorority member who lives in the sorority's house.

In-house legacy: A potential new member whose blood relative (usually a sister) is an active member in one of the sororities the potential member is rushing.

Inactive member: A member who chooses inactive status and has no participation in or influence over sorority activities.

Initiation: The formal ceremony bringing new members officially into the sorority. The events vary as each sorority has its own traditions.

Intentional single preference: Listing only one chapter on a bid card. Sometimes called a *suicide bid* or *"suiciding."*

Interest group: A group on campus in the first stages of the expansion process, before they become installed as members of a sorority.

Lavaliere: A pendant with Greek letters. It's often given by a fraternity member to his girlfriend to signify a serious relationship.

Legacy: The daughter, granddaughter, or sister of a sorority member. Legacy status does not guarantee a bid, but sororities typically like to know if you have legacy status.

Letters: The Greek letters that make up a sorority or fraternity's name.

Mascot: A symbol, usually an animal, chosen to represent a sorority.

Mismatch: When a potential new member's choices don't line up with sororities' choices.

Mixer: A casual social event, held locally and often on a weeknight, with members of a certain sorority and fraternity.

National: A sorority or fraternity's central headquarters. Many sororities and fraternities are actually international, having chapters outside the United States.

The National Association of Latino Fraternal Organizations: Established in 1998, this organization is an umbrella council for Latino Greek Letter Organizations. There are twenty-four member organizations from across the United States. Its Web site is www.nalfo. org.

National Panhellenic Conference: The governing body that oversees sororities. The NPC's Web site (www.npcwomen.org) is a great source for information on sororities' history, alumnae activities, and policies and links to sororities' national Web sites.

National Pan-Hellenic Council: The governing body that oversees historically black fraternities and sororities. Its Web site (www.nphchq. org) has great information about this organization's history and current activities, including alumnae events and philanthropic work.

Neophyte or neo: A new member of an NPHC organization.

New member: Someone who has been offered and has accepted a bid to join a sorority but has not yet been initiated.

New member pin: A badge worn by new members during the time between Bid Day and initiation.

New member class: The group of new pledges who go through the pledge period and initiation together.

New member program: The period after Bid Day and before initiation, when new members learn about their sororities and its active members. Also called the *pledge period*.

Open motto: A sorority or fraternity's publicly stated creed or purpose.

Open recruitment: Informal recruiting without formal scheduled events.

Order of Omega: An academic honor society for Greek members.

Panhellenic: The group that governs sororities. The term means "all Greek."

Philanthropy: A sorority or fraternity's charitable activities.

Pledge: A new member who has been offered and has accepted a bid but has not yet been formally initiated into the chapter.

Pledge Swap: A casual social event with the new members of a certain fraternity and sorority.

Pinning: When a fraternity member gives his pin to his girlfriend.

Potential new member: An individual being considered for membership.

Preferential (Pref): The Preferential Round, the last round in the recruitment process. During this round potential new members visit houses a final time before deciding.

Preference Card: The card a potential new member signs to indicate her final choices just before bids are handed out.

Quota: The target number of new members a sorority is looking to accept.

Recommendation (Rec): A letter written by a sorority alumna on behalf of a girl who is about to go through the recruitment process, sent directly to the sorority she will visit during rush. The letter introduces the girl to the sorority and highlights her good character and academic and civic achievements.

Recruitment counselor: An active sorority member who serves during recruitment as a guide through the process. Her particular affiliation is not advertised so it will not influence potential new members. At some schools this person is called a *Rho Chi*.

Recruitment/rush: The process during which potential members select the sorority that's right for them while sororities choose the members who are right for them.

Reference/letter of recommendation: A letter from an alumna to a sorority on behalf of a potential new member. Sororities often have forms available on their national Web sites with instructions on how they are to be sent.

Retreat: A trip or sleepover where sorority members get to know each other better.

Rituals: Secret ceremonies with significance that are unique to each Greek organization.

Rush/recruitment: The process during which potential members select the sorority that's right for them while sororities choose the members who are right for them.

Semi-formals: Less casual than a *mixer* but not as structured as a *formal*, these are dressy social events usually held locally.

Silence: The policy whereby sorority members and potential members are not to discuss recruitment matters outside of official recruitment events. Your recruitment booklet will have the specifics for your school. If sorority members seem unfriendly during this time it is because they are obeying the rules of silence, not because they're rude!

Sister: A sorority member.

Snap bid: A bid given to a rushee who wasn't matched during the recruitment process. This occurs right after Bid Day proceedings.

Sorority: A Greek-letter organization for women.

Suicide bid: Listing only one chapter on a bid card.

Sweetheart: A woman, usually a sorority member, given special designation by a fraternity.

Theme party: A social event where everyone dresses up in costumes in accordance with the stated theme.

CHAPTER FOUR

Getting It Together:

Your Plan of Action

Getting It Together: Your Plan of Action

It's one thing to look fabulous walking through the door, but when it comes to sorority life, it all starts by looking great on paper. And it starts early. The summer before your freshman year is the home stretch, not the starting block.

To give yourself the best advantage for recruitment, **keep these four Rs in mind and in order: Resume, recommendations, and registration. Then comes recruitment.**

Here's the Four-R Rundown:

Your **resume** is a one-page snapshot of you. It's your academic, extracurricular, and work experience on a page.

You will send your resume to people you ask to write **recommendations** for you. Recommendations are letters from past sorority members on your behalf, sent before recruitment directly to sorority chapters at your college or to the Panhellenic office at your school (check the Web site!). These recommendations introduce you to the sorority before you get there.

Registration is how you sign up for recruitment/rush. Each school has specific requirements, and each school has a deadline. Pay attention to your school's deadline! Miss it, and your next shot at sorority life can be a year away.

Recruitment, which can seem like a week-long interview, is the process of mutual selection where prospective members and sororities make choices to find the best fit.

You'll need to start working two to three months before recruitment. Now let's get you going.

Resumes: Looking Great on Paper

Long before pulling those cute outfits together for your first rush party, you'll need to prepare your resume—basically, a formal list of your academic and extracurricular accomplishments and work activities. The recruitment process is something like a weeklong job interview, and your resume is an opportunity to present yourself before the members meet you. In a few years you'll be putting together similar materials as you head toward the job market or graduate school.

Don't stress if you weren't in a bunch of clubs or didn't make the sports teams during high school. Could it be because you were too busy volunteering with your church youth choir? Because you snagged a really great part-time job where you learned a ton about the career you want to pursue after college? Speak up! Sororities need a snapshot of what you've been up to in the years before college. Your resume is your chance to tell them.

Oh, and before you start getting that paperwork in gear, remember this: Sororities want to know the real you. Make sure what you put in ink is true. Don't even think about making anything up. They will check! You can be sure that someone in the sorority will know someone from your high school who knew you. (It's like Six Degrees of Separation for your high school years.)

You'll first use your resume to provide information for people writing recommendations for you. In many cases, that person will include your resume with the recommendation they send to the sorority.

At many schools, prospective members submit resumes along with application forms. At some, separate resumes are not required, as the registration form you fill out contains information you would list on a resume. Find out what your school requires by checking the Web site. Greek life info is usually on a separate link. If you can't find it look under "Student Life" or "Student Activities." If there's a search function, type in "sorority" or "recruitment." If all else fails, look on the site map—or call the Greek life office and ask.

Sorority members have piles of paperwork to wade through, so try to make yours stand out. (No, not by using scented paper like

Elle Woods in *Legally Blonde*.) Including a unique and interesting accomplishment will help distinguish yours. On some campuses, you'll submit a photograph; this is up to Panhellenic officials at your school. Especially if photos are not part of the application, having a resume that pops can help you connect with members during rush parties. ("Hey, you're the girl who's fluent in four languages," or "I saw you volunteered with the Red Cross during high school.")

SUCCESS STRATEGIES *for Resumes:*

- Make it a one-page snapshot of your academic background, your involvement in clubs and groups, and your unique characteristics.

- Be honest! Don't stretch the truth about your achievements—it's too easy to get busted.

- Keep it neat, concise, and free of errors.

Be aware that having your materials in order is pretty much expected. A sloppy or incomplete resume can make you look bad, but an awesome-looking one isn't really a big bonus, according to an alumna who said, "Everybody looks good on paper. They all over-exaggerate. Positive, well-prepared recs and resumes don't really stick out much, because pretty much everyone has a good-looking resume. It's the sloppy ones we remembered—and not in a good way."

Also, remember the girls in sororities are just a few years removed from high school. If you brag about being valedictorian when really it was a three-way tie and there were only ten graduating seniors in your small, private high school—chances are someone in the sorority knows what the deal is. Anything on your resume is subject to being checked out so make sure it's all legit.

Take time to gather your thoughts before sitting down to fill out your applications and preparing your resume. Write a rough draft (or two) before completing the paperwork. Preparing your resume for recruitment will be great practice for you; in a few years you'll be sending it to prospective employers. Have a parent or other adult you trust proofread your paperwork before you send it in!

A Word from a Wordsmith

Journalist and communications consultant Margot Carmichael Lester is author of "The Real Life Guide to Starting Your Career" (Pipeline Press, 1998) and president of The Word Factory. Her suggestions for getting yourself together on paper:

* Printed letterhead is nice but not essential.

* Use a slightly larger font size for your name.

* Make sure your contact information is current.

* Emphasize your good traits. For example, show your organizational skills and enthusiasm by mentioning you coordinated a charity event at your school or church.

* Keep it short and simple. The sorority members reading your resume will be reading hundreds of others. Don't use a big word when a short one will do. Fussy, formal language doesn't impress anybody, it just takes longer to read.

* Use active verbs. (Instead of saying, "I have been involved in organizing Red

Cross blood drives that have been held at my school," say, "I helped organize my school's Red Cross blood drives.")

✳ Check your spelling and grammar, and don't rely on your computer's spell-check program! Accidentally inserting the suggested replacement your computer offers can produce disastrous results. A spell-check program won't catch correctly spelled words used incorrectly, either.

✳ Have a parent or other adult whose opinion you value review your resume. A fresh pair of eyes may catch a mistake or come up with a good suggestion.

Keep in mind...

Everyone's background is different. One girl might have higher grades, another might have lots of community involvement, while another might have participated in lots of sports activities while holding down part-time jobs. These are all great attributes. Obviously, the more great traits you have, the better. Sororities look for different strengths in their members. Feel confident about yours.

Information on your resume helps sorority members come up with conversation starters during recruitment. For example, Alicia Wilson, our hypothetical rushee whose sample resume you're about to read, played two varsity sports during high school. Her dad is a golf pro and her mom is a tennis coach. Perhaps she'd like to talk about sports interests during rush.

Resume Do's and Don'ts

✓ **Do** use an interesting font – one that's easy to read.

✓ **Do** go beyond basic white for your paper. Stationery and office-supply stores stock high-quality paper in different colors.

✓ **Do** pay attention to your school's requirements. Some schools want photos and others don't. Always include a nice photo of yourself with resumes you provide to people who will be writing recommendations for you.

✗ **Don't** feel like you have to be overly modest. Sorority members will want to know about your leadership roles in school and community groups and what you've accomplished.

✗ **Don't,** repeat, don't, make up even one tiny detail. It is so not worth it. The girls you'll meet during recruitment will likely become lifelong friends. Don't start out that relationship by pretending to be someone you're not.

Your objective is not to fill an entire page—it's to accurately and positively portray yourself. If it seems there are holes in your resume, it's time to get them plugged in! Find a club or activity you love and get involved. Check with your school counselor or faith leader. Log onto www.sororityguide.com for volunteering ideas.

To help you get organized, fill out the Sorority Guide profile sheet on the following page. Take your information and put it into a one- or two-page format. See the following pages for examples or www.sororityguide.com for resume help.

Your turn! See how fab you look in print.

Sorority Guide Profile

NAME
_____

LOCAL ADDRESS
_____

PHONE   EMAIL   BIRTH DATE
_____

EDUCATION
_____

HIGH SCHOOL GRADUATION DATE   HIGH SCHOOL GPA
_____

SAT/ACT SCORE   PLANNED MAJOR   CURRENT GPA
_____

AWARDS, SCHOLARSHIPS
_____

CLUBS – ORGANIZATIONS – SPORTS – ACHIEVEMENTS
_____

WORK EXPERIENCE
_____

PARENTS'/FAMILY GREEK AFFILIATION (OPTIONAL)

Check out these examples and www.sororityguide. com for help:

ALICIA WILSON

123 Bryant Way
Every City, USA 12345
105-555-2345
awilson@ecity.com

BIRTH DATE:	August 23, 1988
COLLEGE INFORMATION:	State University, class of 2010
	567 Smith Dorm
	Planned major: Communications
HIGH SCHOOL:	Greenville High School
	Graduation date: May 2006
	GPA: 2.8
	ACT score: 27
AWARDS:	Civic pride essay contest,
	second place, 2005
	Lettered in softball, 2004–2006
CLUBS:	Boys and Girls Club
	Relay for Life team, 2004–2006
	American Red Cross blood drive
VARSITY SPORTS:	Soccer, softball
WORK EXPERIENCE:	Part-time assistant technician at local
	Humane Society
PARENTS:	Brent Wilson, City College, 1974
	Occupation: Golf pro
	Trish Wilson, State Junior College, 1978
	Occupation: Tennis coach

Lindsay Robson

567 West Maple Street, Any Town, USA 56789
919-555-5678 • lindsayrob@atown.com

College:

Big State University, 123 Jones Dorm
Class Entering: Freshman (Fall 2005)
Planned Major: Education

High School:

Piedmont Girls School
GPA: 3.7 (on 4.0 scale); Graduation date: May 2005
SAT score: 1950 (out of 2400)

Birth Date: March 16, 1987

Achievements, Awards, Scholarships Offices Held:

National Scholars Program award winner, 2005
Sophomore class treasurer, 2004
Spanish Club secretary, 2003

Clubs and Organizations:

Debate Club, 2003
Honor Society, 2005
Youth Missions Team member, 2004–05
Youth choir, 2001–05

Work Experience:

Part-time teacher's aide, Grace Church nursery, 2003–2004

Parents:

Jerry Robson, VP, IEC Corp., University College 1965,
Lambda Delta fraternity
Catherine Robson, Children's Director, Grace Church,
State College, 1968, Alpha Beta sorority

BOTTOM LINE:

Sororities aren't looking for members who are perfect in every way — they don't exist. Organize and highlight your info to show off your best self.

Recommendations: What's Up with Recs?

Recommendations (recs) are letters of reference on your behalf from alumnae sorority members, sent to the sororities you will visit during recruitment. At most schools they are helpful but not absolutely required. The members of each sorority decide how much importance to place on paperwork, including recommendations. It's different for each chapter of each sorority on each campus, and there's really no way for you to know what each sorority's deal is.

Technically it is up to the sorority to get a recommendation on each new member, but don't make them work too hard for you! If you get your recs together, that's one task the sorority doesn't have to do. There are so many girls for them to choose from—don't fall through the cracks because you made more work for the members.

Do know many girls come in with at least one rec for every sorority they are interested in. Often they'll have more than one. If you can, send at least one recommendation to each sorority. You never know which sorority will really interest you until you meet the members.

SUCCESS STRATEGIES *for Recs:*

For informal rush, your school info doesn't address recs: one rec per sorority.

For formal rush, your school info indicates recs are a good idea but isn't specific: two recs per sorority.

For competitive rush, your school has a large number of girls rushing: try for three recs per sorority.

Sororities usually have rec forms (sometimes they are called sponsor forms), on their Web sites, generally in the "members only" section. The site will have instructions on how recommendations should be sent.

To begin assembling recs, log onto your school's Web site. Make a list of sorority chapters at your school. List anyone you know who was a member of one of these sororities. Organize your list of potential recommendation writers. (For guidance log onto www.sororityguide. com and look for the rec link.)

Where do you find the women who will write recs for you? If you have a family member or family friend who was a member of a sorority, request a recommendation. If it's someone you personally don't know all that well, like one of your mother's friends, get to know her! Prepare a rec package (details later) to help this person get an idea of your background. She'll be able to write a much more effective letter of recommendation once she knows you and has the info.

The sorority will want to know how that person knows you or is related to you, and why she feels you would be a good fit for the sorority. The letter might give examples of your leadership in the community, academic performance, special talents or interests, and general character.

Recommendations can come from relatives or friends, or from someone who doesn't know you but has reviewed your resume, such as a friend of a friend. The most effective recommendation will be from someone who knows you personally and was a member of the exact chapter you are rushing. Not many girls will have such specific recs, so don't worry if you don't. Recs from relatives who were sorority members elsewhere are also helpful. Then come those from personal friends who were sorority members. The key is the personal relationship. Effective recommendations reveal how the writer knows you and why she can personally vouch for your character.

The best recommendation gives the sorority some basic information about you. It might include:

- Your high school rank, activities and interests, planned major at college, and work or volunteer history.
- How the person knows you and how long she's known you.
- Your special talents, academic honors or community involvement, awards and honors.
- Your parents' community involvement and Greek affiliations.
- Greek affiliations of other relatives.
- How you would make a positive contribution to the sorority.

Where are recommendations sent? That depends on the college. Contact the Panhellenic office at your school to learn where letters of recommendation should be sent and the deadline by which they must be received. Sororities on your campus will have information posted on their Web sites as well. This will provide the addresses to which recommendations should be sent, and the person to whose attention they should be directed.

You don't have friends or relatives who were in sororities? No problem—here are some success strategies for you:

- Start asking around and networking! Ladies in your church or synagogue, your teachers, or your parents' friends or colleagues could be good resources.

- Contact the local Panhellenic or collegiate alumnae group in your area. Check out the National Panhellenic Web site, www. npcwomen.org, for help with recs.

- Get to know people you meet for the purpose of writing a recommendation well ahead of your deadline so they can write you an effective letter.

- If you do have a number of people willing to write recommendations for you, ask yourself: How can I get the best possible letter of recommendation? Whom should I ask to write one? When should I ask her to write it?

The Recommendation Package

Once you have identified people who are willing to recommend you to sororities, you need to put together your recommendations package for them. Your rec package should include:

- A request letter asking the person to recommend you (example follows). Your letter should include information on how, when, and where to send the recommendation to your school. If the sororities at your school want them snail-mailed, include a stamped, addressed envelope. If they prefer email, include the email address. Let the writer know the deadline by which the recommendation must be sent.

Other items to include in your package:

▪ Your completed resume (by now you're looking great on paper).

▪ Your photograph, which can be your senior high school picture. It doesn't have to be a professional photograph, just a nice picture that shows your best self. Write your name on the back.

▪ A copy of your school transcript.

Don't forget to say thank you! Make a note on your calendar to send a handwritten thank-you note about ten days after you send the recommendation package. Not only is this good manners, it also may remind the writer if she has been too busy to drop it in the mail for you.

You must be extremely organized. See www.sororityguide.com for more great tools to help you keep it all together.

The Request Letter

Here's an example of a note you might send to a family friend requesting she write a letter of recommendation for you:

Amy Gardner
123 Jamestown Way
Any Town, Any State 12345

June 1, 2005

Dear Mrs. Baker,

I enjoyed seeing you and your family at the beach over spring break. We always have so much fun together.

I appreciate your offer to help me with sorority recruitment by writing a letter of recommendation to Delta Alpha Sorority. I have included my high school transcript and resume. The recommendation should be received by August 1. Recruitment begins on August 15.

I have also enclosed a stamped envelope addressed to Delta Alpha Sorority. The web site is www.deltaalpha.com.

Thanks so much for all your help. I look forward to visiting with you before I leave for school.

Sincerely,

Amy Gardner

The Rec Thank You

It's very important to follow up with a thank-you note to people who have agreed to write recommendations for you. Send the thank you note about ten days after you have sent the recommendation package (letter requesting the recommendation and your resume and transcript). The thank you note serves as a "gentle reminder" in case the recommendation hasn't yet been sent. It also shows you have good manners.

Here's an example of a thank-you note:

June 25, 2005

Dear Mrs. Baker,

Thanks again for writing the letter of recommendation for me to the Delta Alpha Sorority. I am very excited about recruitment and will let you know what happens.

I look forward to seeing you and your family over the July 4th weekend. I hope you enjoy the rest of the summer.

Sincerely,
Amy Gardner

Avoiding a Rec Wreck:
Do's and Don'ts for Recommendations

✓ **Do** start early. Organize your list of potential recommendation writers. Get the word out that you'll be participating in recruitment.

✓ **Do** network! Friends, neighbors, teachers, employers, coaches —all these people can write recommendations for you.

- ✓ **Do** get it together! Rounding up recommendations is a multi-step process that requires more than a phone call.

- ✓ **Do** remember to thank those people who have supported you as you prepare for recruitment.

- ✗ **Don't** go crazy rounding up recs. Don't think, "The more recs I get to a sorority, the more the sorority is going to like me." One or two strong letters from people who know you well are better than five or six letters from people who really don't know you.

- ✗ **Don't** wait until the last minute to request letters of recommendation. You should be thinking about who to ask for a rec in the early part of your senior year, so that person will have time to write a really meaningful one for you.

- ✗ **Don't** just get your mom to call a friend who knows someone who was in that sorority. Instead, get to know the person yourself. How lame does this sound: "Dear Sorority, I have never even met this girl, but I'm sure she'd work out great..." That's almost worst than no rec at all! Take the time to "sell" yourself if you don't know the rec writer so she can do a good job "selling" you.

- ✗ **Don't** forget to have someone proof your paperwork!

BOTTOM LINE:

Recommendations are one part of the process you can control. Start early, stay organized, and get it done!

Registration: It's all about the form and getting it in on time.

Registration and recruitment are handled through your school's Panhellenic office. Information mailed to you from your college will explain the process. If you feel clueless, seek answers from your school's Web site. Realize that sororities are private organizations that started as secret societies. Detailed information about the recruitment process at some schools may be sketchy.

You may receive information on recruitment and registration in the mail or you may find it on your college's Web site. If you don't see a link to "Greek life" or "Panhellenic" on your school's Web site, do a search on the site for the words "Greek" or "sorority" or "recruitment." Call the Panhellenic or Greek life office if you need help.

Once you find this information, spend time reading it. Look at the pictures. Can you see yourself there?

What to Do and When to Do It

Your school's Web site will have information on when recruitment application materials need to be submitted, or the information may be mailed to you. For fall recruitment, registration usually happens in early July. For spring recruitment, you'll need to have your registration completed before Winter Break begins. Turning in registration materials past the deadline could prevent you from participating in recruitment or you could end up paying a steep late fee.

Be on the lookout for invitations to informational meetings organized by your school or local sorority alumnae. These would be held the summer before freshman year if recruitment is held in the fall, or on your campus if it's held second semester.

Go to your school's Web site or call the Greek life or Panhellenic office, to find out when recruitment is and what the deadline is for registration. Aim to get your materials in at least two weeks before the deadline. Remember that on the other end of that mailing address are sorority members about to be buried alive in paper. Give them a break by getting yours in early.

Treat the registration form like your college application. You'll likely be submitting it on-line, but print it out and proofread carefully before hitting "send."

When filling out your registration, expect to be asked about:

○ Your academic record (the high school you attended, your SAT or ACT scores, any academic honors or awards).

○ Your interests and extracurricular activities, including church, civic, or community involvement and sports teams.

○ Whether your mother, sisters, or grandmothers were members of a sorority.

○ What you want out of your sorority experience, and what you feel you can bring to a chapter.

○ Your special talents, especially those that could play a role in your sorority experience.

○ Leadership qualities, and examples of how you've exhibited those qualities.

○ Work experience.

○ Any special needs you might have during the recruitment process. If you've broken your ankle and will be on crutches during rush, let everyone know ahead of time.

Sample Registration Form

Sarah Somebody   _ssomebody@server.com_
NAME   E-MAIL ADDRESS

_123-45-6789_   _February 14, 1987_
SOCIAL SECURITY NUMBER   DATE OF BIRTH

123 Main Street, Anytown USA, 12345
HOME ADDRESS

456 Johnson Dorm, Collegetown USA, 54321
LOCAL/CAMPUS ADDRESS

_205-555-1234_
LOCAL/CAMPUS PHONE NUMBER

Great Big High, Anytown, USA   _June 10, 2005_
HIGH SCHOOL ATTENDED   DATE OF HIGH SCHOOL GRADUATION

_3.3_   _1500_
HIGH SCHOOL GPA   SAT SCORE

THIS FALL YOU WILL BE A: ☑ FRESHMAN ☐ SOPHOMORE ☐ TRANSFER STUDENT
☐ OTHER (LIST)_____

n/a (Sarah is a freshman and doesn't yet have college credit).
IF APPLICABLE, COLLEGE GPA AND NUMBER OF CREDIT HOURS COMPLETED

_n/a_
IF APPLICABLE, PREVIOUS COLLEGE YOU ATTENDED/GPA FROM THAT COLLEGE

National Honor Society Member
Three AP classes senior year; two AP classes junior year
OTHER COMMENTS REGARDING YOUR ACADEMIC RECORD (SCHOLARSHIPS, ETC.)

_No_   _No_
HAVE YOU PARTICIPATED IN RECRUITMENT AT THIS SCHOOL?   ANOTHER SCHOOL?

Mother (Sally Somebody, maiden name Sally Usedtobe) w
State University, Sister (Sherry Somebody) was an ΣΦΓ a
ARE YOU RELATED TO ANY SORORITY MEMBERS?

Rotary Club Civic Essay Contest Winner,
City League Volunteer Award, Science and math achievem
ACADEMIC, CIVIC, OR COMMUNITY HONORS YOU HAVE RECEIVED:

All-State Chorus, Youth League volunteer member
LEADERSHIP ROLES – INVOLVEMENT IN CLUBS – CHURCH – OTHE

_____
LEADERSHIP ROLES – INVOLVEMENT IN CLUBS – CHURCH – OTH

I play the piano and sing soprano.
SPECIAL INTERESTS, TALENTS

I love meeting new people, I have always enjoyed volunteering with projects in
my hometown, and I want to meet girls who have similar interests and goals.
I will be an enthusiastic, involved member dedicated to my sorority and its
members.
WHY YOU WANT TO JOIN A SORORITY, WHAT YOU FEEL YOU CAN BRING?

None
ANY SPECIAL NEEDS DURING RECRUITMENT?

If yes to either, the form may ask for details: whether you were previously a member of a sorority, if you dropped out of recruitment and why, etc.

Your turn! Here's a practice form, to help you pull yourself together on the page.

NAME   E-MAIL ADDRESS

SOCIAL SECURITY NUMBER   DATE OF BIRTH

HOME ADDRESS

LOCAL/CAMPUS ADDRESS

LOCAL/CAMPUS PHONE NUMBER

HIGH SCHOOL ATTENDED   DATE OF HIGH SCHOOL GRADUATION

HIGH SCHOOL GPA   SAT SCORE

THIS FALL YOU WILL BE A: ☐ FRESHMAN ☐ SOPHOMORE ☐ TRANSFER STUDENT ☐ OTHER (LIST)_____

IF APPLICABLE, COLLEGE GPA AND NUMBER OF CREDIT HOURS COMPLETED

IF APPLICABLE, PREVIOUS COLLEGE YOU ATTENDED/GPA FROM THAT COLLEGE

OTHER COMMENTS REGARDING YOUR ACADEMIC RECORD (SCHOLARSHIPS, ETC.)

HAVE YOU PARTICIPATED IN RECRUITMENT AT THIS SCHOOL?   ANOTHER SCHOOL?

ARE YOU RELATED TO ANY SORORITY MEMBERS?

ACADEMIC, CIVIC, OR COMMUNITY HONORS YOU HAVE RECEIVED:

LEADERSHIP ROLES – INVOLVEMENT IN CLUBS – CHURCH – OTHER ORGANIZATIONS

LEADERSHIP ROLES – INVOLVEMENT IN CLUBS – CHURCH – OTHER ORGANIZATIONS

SPECIAL INTERESTS, TALENTS

WHY YOU WANT TO JOIN A SORORITY, WHAT YOU FEEL YOU CAN BRING?

ANY SPECIAL NEEDS DURING RECRUITMENT?

Note: You'll probably be asked to sign a certification that everything you have listed is accurate.

Registration Do's and Don'ts

- ✓ **Do** know the deadline and meet it!
- ✓ **Do** carefully review the Greek information on your school's Web site.
- ✓ **Do** proofread everything and proofread it again.
- ✓ **Do** have a copy of your official school transcript from the year prior to recruitment. Be prepared to send a number of copies —they will be provided to the individual chapters.
- ✗ **Don't** send your photograph unless it is specifically requested.
- ✗ **Don't** be late—it could cost you more than money.
- ✗ **Don't** be sloppy.

BOTTOM LINE:
_____

Your registration needs to be neat, complete, and on time.

What to Do When: Your Recruitment Timeline and To Do Lists

You shouldn't wait until the last minute to get ready for recruitment. To feel the most confident and prepared, it's a good idea to start early. Here are some tips to get you ready, and space for you to put your plan in writing. Get it going!

The final months of your senior year in high school will be hectic —events like your spring break, senior prom, and graduation will keep you super busy, and senioritis may tempt you to do little besides talk on your cell phone. Make sure you find time to get recruitment materials together.

If you applied for early decision, you may know where you're going to college before the winter holidays. Sweet! You can use the break to round up your recommendations, or at least to contact people who would be good to ask later. Remember the best recommendations are ones from people who actually know you. The earlier you can start making contacts with future rec writers, the better.

If you won't find out until the second semester of your senior year where you're going to school, it's even more important to get your act together. As soon as you know, find out which sororities are on the campus you're headed to, and give a shout out to alumnae you know are willing to write recs.

Eighteen months to two years prior: Work on becoming the best candidate you can be! Olympic athletes don't wait until two weeks before the Games to start training—and you're not waiting until the last month of your senior year to start applying to college, right? The earlier you get involved in clubs or sports activities, the better. Consider volunteering with Habitat for Humanity, the United Way, the Humane Society, or groups supported by your church or synagogue. Don't wait to start worrying about grades at the last minute, either.

What are you up to now? How are your grades? What could you do to improve your academic and social standing?

18 months to 2 years prior (Sophomore Year)

*　_____

　_____

*　_____

　_____

*　_____

　_____

　_____

Twelve to eighteen months prior: You found some activities you loved and some you didn't, and ended up with the best fit. That is just what you'll do during recruitment! During this time, it's important to start really thinking about what you want out of a sorority experience, and what you think you could add to a sorority.

So how about it? Why do you want to go Greek? What benefits do you feel sorority life holds for you, and what can you contribute?

12 to 18 months prior (Junior Year)

_____

_____

_____

_____

_____

_____

_____

_____

Six to twelve months prior: You've gotten your thoughts together by now and you're ready to rush! Your senior year is going to be amazing—in both good and stressful ways. You'll be taking the SAT (numerous times, maybe), applying to colleges, waiting on those acceptance letters, and deciding where you're headed for school. Once you've made up your mind, check out the Greek scene on your campus. Now is the time to start asking people if they would consider writing recommendations for you. You should also learn something about the different sororities on your campus. The college Web site will have information about their social and service activities. Sororities' national Web sites have information about their history, philanthropic goals, and fun facts like how they picked their badge design.

Which sororities have chapters on your campus-to-be? Whom will you ask for letters of recommendation? Make a list.

6 to 12 months prior (Senior Year)

Three to six months prior: You know a little about the sororities at your college. You've attended informational meetings sponsored by alumnae in your town. You've found some great ladies to write recs for you. Now is the time to start getting ready to submit all your paperwork. Find out where registration forms, resumes, and recommendations should be sent and what the deadlines are. If sororities on your campus want photos submitted with applications, think about getting them together now. Your senior photo or a fun snapshot will be fine, just make sure you have enough prints. It's good to have extras in case some get lost or damaged. You should start getting your recruitment wardrobe together (see our fashion advice in Chapter 6!), and decide if you're going to wear your hair long, get it chopped, do highlights, or try a new style. There's time to let it grow out if you decide you don't like it.

When is your paperwork due? What are you wearing for recruitment?

3 to 6 months prior (Senior Year)

✓

✓

✓

TO DO...

One to three months prior: Send recommendation packages to the people you've asked to write letters of recommendation for you. The package should include a personal letter requesting the recommendation, your resume, photo, transcript, and stamped envelopes properly addressed to the Greek life office for mailing. Your paperwork needs to be turned in to your college, along with recruitment fees and photos, if requested.

You should definitely know what you're wearing to each round. If you don't already have your outfits, get busy! This is the time to start breaking in those cute new shoes, so they feel great when it's time to wear them all day walking from house to house.

Have you sent out your rec packages? Have you turned everything in? Do you have all your clothes picked out and ready to go?

1 to 3 months prior

* _____

* _____

* _____

TO DO...

Two to four weeks prior: You may be packing to leave for college or getting ready for the new term at school. Either way, there's a lot going on. But don't forget to send thank-you notes to everyone who wrote letters of recommendation for you.

Your recruitment outfits need to be cleaned, pressed, and ready to wear. Take everything to a good dry cleaner so details like minor alterations or a missing button can be fixed. Get your hair cut (and highlighted), and get your brows waxed. To be sure you'll feel confident through every round of recruitment, come up with some "talking points" about yourself. What you were up to during high school? What cool talents and interests do you have? Also, come up with a list of five questions to ask girls you'll meet during rush. You'll be asking and answering the same questions at each chapter—get ready!

What do you still need to do? What are your talking points? What five questions will you ask?

2 to 4 weeks prior

TO DO...

One week prior: Get a manicure and try to relax! Review your thoughts about sorority life and why you're taking this journey. Jot down some thoughts to answer these questions: Why should I choose a sorority? Why should a sorority choose me?

1 week prior

✓ _____

✓ _____

✓ _____

_____

_____

_____

TO DO...

BOTTOM LINE:

You've gotten it together, and you look great in print. You're feeling confident, pumped, and ready. It's time to get your game on!

CHAPTER FIVE

What's the Rush?

What's the Rush?

A sorority is a cross-section of girls with different interests and backgrounds working toward common goals. They find their new members through the recruitment process. They call it "recruitment" in all the official materials, but people still call it "rush." You meet the sorority members, they meet you, everyone chooses the best fit, and a new pledge class is born.

The first step in your recruitment process is to answer this question: Do I want to be in a sorority? Once you have decided that you definitely want to pursue Greek life, your next challenge is to remain open minded. Set a goal for recruitment to find two or three sororities that you'll feel comfortable in.

Every sorority, every sorority chapter, and each sorority member is different. Through the years, sororities often pick up certain labels —one is known as the "athletic girls' sorority," another is where all the former beauty queens are, yet another is home to all the 4.0 girls. Don't be ruled by rumors, but do investigate and observe what's important to each chapter. Here, Web sites can give you clues. Sites might proudly display chapter awards, average GPAs, or social activities. Think about what's important to you as you learn more about each chapter. It'll help you make the best connection.

Every recruitment process is different, too. Details specific to your school will be available on your college's Web site, and you may be mailed a packet of recruitment information. Do not throw anything away that comes from your college. You can be sure the one envelope you thought wasn't important enough to keep will be the one with all the information you'll need.

It's up to you to familiarize yourself with your school's rush process. Recruitment is held at different times during the year at different schools. Some schools hold recruitment the week prior to classes, some the week classes begin, and some a few weeks after classes have started. At some schools, rush isn't held until the second term.

Here's the good news: most of the girls participating in recruitment end up pledging a sorority. We've experienced rush ourselves, and we've interviewed tons of girls at various schools across the country for an inside look at recruitment. Here's a look at the various types:

Fall: Recruitment held before classes begin.

Spring/winter: Recruitment held before the beginning of second term or semester

Deferred: Any formal recruitment process after school begins. This can include:

- **Fall semester** after classes begin
- **Snap bidding:** When a sorority elects to fill slots that remain, and offer bids to girls who did not find a match during the recruitment process. This happens immediately following the recruitment process, often within minutes.
- **Open recruitment/continuous open bidding**: When a sorority has open slots for whatever reason and elects to fill them after the formal recruitment ends. This begins after the snap bidding process concludes.

Pay attention to everything your college mails to you at home and to information on the school's Web site. The materials will likely include a recruitment booklet with dates, deadlines, and examples of resumes, registration forms, and other forms.

Here's what you can expect during recruitment

You'll get to town. Your school will provide information on housing during recruitment, whether on campus or elsewhere. You'll meet the other girls participating in recruitment. There may be an organizational meeting before the process begins. If there is, we highly recommend you attend.

You'll meet the counselor who will advise you throughout recruitment. These girls sometimes go by Greek letters that do not have any affiliation with sororities on that campus. (Rho Chi and Chi Phi are some names for recruitment counselors, but at some schools the girls don't use Greek letters). Your recruitment counselor will advise you during the process, collect your bid cards, return with the list of sororities you're invited back to visit, and generally keep you from melting down. To avoid influencing you, they can't wear their letters, and they can't talk to anyone about their sororities. They usually have to move out of the house or hall if they live there.

Your counselor will be a great resource during recruitment, but she is not there to give her opinion on sororities or which one you should join. Her job is to help you through the process so that you can make the best decision for yourself.

Advice from Girls Who Have Been There

"I was going to be myself. My heart wasn't set on it. Therefore I wasn't trying too hard. Going in without expectations made it easier. My rush experience went well. I ended up having a lot of fun with it."

– a sophomore sorority member

"It was not fun. It was the longest week. But it was worth it!"

– a sorority alumnae member

SUCCESS STRATEGY to Get You Started:
No Drama!

The official rush events take place at specific times and places. You'll also have some down time to relax. Be on your best behavior throughout recruitment. Bad manners are never acceptable, but this is certainly not the time to throw a fit in the campus dining hall because the line's too long, or cop an attitude in the campus bookstore because your required textbook is out of stock. You'll probably be worn out by the end of each day; even if you're not, don't hit the downtown clubs with a fake ID. You never know who might be watching. It could be one of the girls who decides whether you get a bid or not.

Round-by-Round

There are typically four rounds during the recruitment process. Here's a round-by-round look at what you can expect. We've compiled the best "do's and don'ts" from current and former sorority members from schools across the country. And, we've got lists of sample questions for you to consider during each round. There's space for you to start jotting some of your own questions and comments for each round.

A note on the vote: Actives in each sorority vote at the conclusion of each round of recruitment. They typically come up with three categories: definite yes, definite no, and girls to talk about. The list of prospective members is ranked and submitted to campus Panhellenic officials. Sororities' choices and rushees' choices are run through a computer to produce the next day's list of invitations.

We're here to help you stay in the running throughout the process! Let's look at details on each round and a typical recruitment schedule.

A Closer Look at Each Round

A round in the recruitment process is the series of parties held each particular day; at some schools, with many sororities, the first round can last two days. All sororities on a campus follow the same round schedule.

There may be three to five rounds of rush; the most typical recruitment schedule includes four rounds. During round one, often called ice-water tea or open house, you'll spend time with each sorority, getting an overall sense of each one. The purpose of round one is to give both sides an initial face-to-face meeting to begin looking for potential connections. At schools where sororities have houses, you'll visit the members there during the rounds. At schools where sororities do not have houses, rush may be held in the student center or specific locations, such as chapter rooms in dorm buildings.

Round two is usually the house tour or philanthropy day. On philanthropy day, you'll make a simple craft with the aid of sorority members that will be donated to charity. Sisters lead prospective new members through their houses during house tours, pointing out amenities like study lounges, parlors, and dining rooms along with bedrooms.

Round three is often skit day, where sisters put their dramatic skills to work teaching potential new members about their sorority.

Round four, preferential day, is a serious, often emotional round as you and the sororities make final choices. This is when you express your final preference.

The final step of recruitment is bid day, when sororities meet their new sisters!

RUSH SCHEDULE

Round 1   Open House

Round 2   Philanthropy Day

Round 3   Skit Day

Round 4   Preferential Day

Bid Day

Round One: The First Impression (Open House)

The first day of rush will be busy! Everyone participating in recruitment will be invited to all sororities. You will visit every sorority on campus, spending fifteen to twenty minutes at each one. Depending on how your campus is organized, you'll either walk or ride buses to the different houses. You'll be in a large group during the first round of rush. At colleges where rush is held prior to classes, you'll be getting up very early every day. Prepare for a long day by eating breakfast. Have your clothes and everything you need to get dressed set out the night before. Carry a bag with Band-Aids, safety pins, breath mints, and comfy shoes.

Excitement mounts inside the house as the first group of rushees arrives. The active members have spent months preparing for you, and they are pumped! They will have spent many hours going over skits, deciding what to wear each day, and what everyone's role will be for rush. The sorority's leadership will have encouraged the girls to touch up their manicures and hair and the house will have been cleaned from top to bottom in anticipation of rush. Believe it or not, the sisters are just as nervous as you are—maybe even more so. They are looking for their new group of sisters, and they can't wait to meet all the new girls.

Before you begin your first rush party, take a mental time-out. Close your eyes for just a second, and visualize a very special moment (the time you landed a super summer job, your first great kiss, the birthday when your parents gave you the puppy you'd been begging for —anything that puts a genuine smile on your face). Hold that feeling. It will help you project confidence and warmth when meeting new people.

The first rush parties often kick off with a cheer or a song welcoming you to each chapter. It can be amazingly loud! The sisters are often nervous themselves and the louder they sing and cheer, the easier it is to keep up their energy levels. After their near-deafening opening acts the sisters will approach the potential members and lead them off for brief conversations. These first contacts are crucial —they're your first impression of each sorority, and each sorority's impression of you. You might talk to another member or two during this first round, but you would never be joined by a big group of girls. Piling too many members on one prospect or otherwise pressuring potential new members is called "hot boxing," and it is not allowed.

The first girl you meet could very well be your "talent agent" throughout rush. If you make a good impression on her and really click during that first conversation, she could be the one pulling for you when it seems like all the great girls are getting cut because there just aren't enough spots. Give her the tools she needs to sell you to her sisters—make her want to work for you. If you don't click with the first girl—don't worry! There are many girls in each chapter. You'll have many opportunities to find a girl you connect with.

Keep in mind, you're going to talk about the same things over and over again at each chapter. Where you're from, which dorm you live in, what you're planning to major in, what activities you're into—all are common conversation topics in this round. Also keep in mind that the greatest number of cuts are made after the first round. Have you heard the song "The First Cut is the Deepest"? That sentiment applies. This is when sororities must make the largest number of cuts, and it's often a relatively superficial process. They make these decisions based on rushees' grades, how they look on paper, and how they present themselves. This round will end quickly. You may feel you didn't meet many members, but it's time to touch up your lip gloss and move on.

After you leave each round-one party, sororities have about fifteen or twenty minutes to prepare for the next group. They'll use this time to straighten up the house, check their makeup and hair, and generally get ready to go again. They'll also make notes about the girls they've just met. Later, they'll refer to these notes when deciding whom to invite back for the next round.

As you leave, choose one word that describes how you felt after leaving each sorority in round one. This will help later when you're trying to collect your thoughts. Remember, this is your experience. Don't pay too much attention to what others think.

Do's and Don'ts for Round One

- ✓ **Do** maintain eye contact and ask questions. Sorority members want active, involved new sisters. Demonstrate you're that kind of girl by showing interest and enthusiasm from the beginning.

- ✓ **Do** be honest if you're nervous or excited. If you lost a button on your top and had to safety pin it shut, laugh it off and move on.

- ✓ **Do** ask questions that indicate genuine interest about the sorority and sorority life.

- ✓ **Do** come up with a few conversation topics you can use with anyone. (Review the *Sorority Guide* sample questions in the following section for ideas!) You really want to avoid dead air time.

- ✗ **Don't** ask if boys are allowed upstairs in the sorority house. They're not.

- ✗ **Don't** label yourself a party girl by asking questions like, "Do they card much here?" or "Do they check IDs at your formals and mixers?"

- ✗ **Don't** play the name game. (This includes your boyfriend.) Don't take the chance, no matter how remote, of bringing up ancient drama. .

- ✗ **Don't** swear. This doesn't make you sound cool. You want to come across polished.

- ✗ **Don't** cross your arms, yawn, roll your eyes, or slouch. Body language speaks volumes about you. Members other than the girl you're talking to may be watching.

Conversation Starters for Round One

So what are you going to talk about? You won't have much time so make yourself memorable by asking questions beyond the common ones (Where are you from? What's your major?) Here are some sample conversation starters.

1. "How did you choose your song or cheer?"

2. Instead of, "Where are you from?" ask, "How did you decide to come to school here?"

3. "Do you live in the house or on the sorority hall?"

4. "How long has XY had a chapter here?"

5. "What committees have you been on?"

Your turn! Come up with some questions so you won't be at a loss for words!

QUESTIONS FOR ROUND 1

1. _____

_____

2. _____

_____

3. _____

_____

4. _____

_____

5. _____

_____

SUCCESS STRATEGY Talk about what you know. You'll be more interesting and feel more comfortable if you're talking about something familiar.

NOTES ON ROUND 1

BOTTOM LINE:

Be real, be genuine, be yourself. That's the key to finding your best fit.

Round Two: Learning More (House Tour or Philanthropy Day)

After you've completed round one (it may take two days, depending on how many sororities your school has) you will rank your choices of sororities you'd like to return to. Using a computer program, Panhellenic Council members match your choices with the list of girls each sorority has chosen to invite back. The sororities' choices drive this match-making process. Your recruitment counselor will deliver the lists to you each day, or tell you where to obtain them.

After round one, sororities must release a certain number of girls. Every round from here on is by invitation only. Some girls get cut based on grades or because of incomplete paperwork. In other cases girls who are cut just didn't make a connection. Our advice? Try not to take getting cut personally. The elimination process is a necessary numbers game. Your recruitment counselor is there for you if you need help dealing with the process.

On philanthropy day, you'll work on a simple craft as you find out about each sorority's signature charity. This is when you will learn about requirements for working on philanthropic events. It is generally a casual round; you'll often be given a T-shirt from the Panhellenic office to wear on this day. It's a good time to start figuring out which sorority's goals and causes most closely match your own. Because you're engaged in an activity, you'll have the opportunity for a more relaxed conversation with sorority members and fellow rushees.

You may or may not see the sorority members you were paired with during the first round. If you happen to spot someone you met earlier, however, it's fine to smile and say hello. The first girl you met at the first rush party may be the one who pushes for you to be invited back, so make every contact count.

During these rounds you'll also get a sense of the time and financial commitments a sorority requires. Along with dues and fees, there are charges for social events and the T-shirts that accompany them.

During house tours, you'll be guided through the house as members point out its features and history.

Do's and Don'ts for Round Two

✓ **Do** realize a main function of a sorority is to raise money for its signature charity. Share information about yourself that shows you can help meet the sorority's charitable goals.

✓ **Do** relax and keep an open mind! You'll be engaged in a fun activity or learning more about the chapter houses. Let your personality shine!

✓ **Do** ask about the charitable goals of the sorority, and about previous fundraisers and philanthropic events. Ask how the sorority chose its signature charity.

✓ **Do** ask questions that indicate you're interested. Sorority houses usually have portraits of their founders prominently displayed. Ask about them. Compliment something about the house, like its dramatic staircase, elegant chandelier, or unique architecture.

✗ **Don't** gossip as you travel between houses with your fellow potential new members. Remember, these are your potential sorority sisters, too.

✗ **Don't** compare one house with another during tours. Saying something like, "Your house is so amazing. It's prettier than the XYZ House," is a terrible idea, even if it's meant as a compliment. You don't want to compare houses—and you never want to say anything bad about any sorority or the rush process.

✗ **Don't** talk only to the active sorority members. Talk with your fellow rushees, too. It's a good way to demonstrate your interest in others and meet girls who could end up in your pledge class.

✗ **Don't** worry about "secret gestures" during rush. Yes, they exist, but you have enough to handle right now. Take every girl for who she is, and treat her with genuine respect.

Conversation Starters for Round Two

By now you understand how important it is to make a connection. Here are some questions to help you.

1. "How did the sorority choose its signature charity?"

2. "What's your favorite thing to do in the house (or chapter room)?"

3. "How many hours a month do you spend on volunteer projects?"

4. "When was this house built? Who originally lived here?" Or, "When did this become your chapter room?"

5. "What is your favorite charitable activity?"

Your turn! Come up with some questions or comments for the house tour or philanthropy day.

QUESTIONS FOR ROUND 2

1. _____

_____

2. _____

_____

3. _____

_____

4. _____

_____

5. _____

_____

SUCCESS STRATEGY Continue your word association, coming up with one word that best describes your feelings about each chapter. No matter how you feel, remember to be polite to everyone you meet.

NOTES ON ROUND 2

_____

_____

_____

_____

_____

_____

_____

_____

_____

_____

_____

BOTTOM LINE:

Relax and enjoy the activities
as you learn what community service
means to each sorority you visit.

Round Three: Get More Involved (Skit Day)

By this round you're spending more time at each chapter and are visiting fewer chapters. This round is about quality time, not quantity. This is many girls' favorite round. The purpose of this round is to share detailed history on the sorority. It can be something of a sales pitch, where the members do their best to show how much fun their chapter is to belong to.

The sorority members will use a funny skit to teach the prospective members more about them and their sorority.

Refreshments are often served during this round. Have some! The girls don't want to have to wrap up hundreds of untouched brownies after you leave. If you feel self-conscious about eating in front of others, select items that can be quickly eaten in one bite.

The selection process continues, and cutting becomes more difficult on both sides. Sororities have no choice, because they can only take a limited number of new members.

There is not as much talking during this round, as the members will use much of the time allotted to entertain you. Afterward, you've got plenty of material to discuss. It's a good opportunity to catch your breath and relax a little.

By this round, if you truly feel no connection to the process or the girls you've met, take some time to re-evaluate whether or not Greek life is for you. Don't feel like you have to wait until the very end. Also keep in mind that disappointments can occur throughout recruitment, not just at the end. It can really hurt if you are cut from a sorority where you felt a connection. Prepare yourself emotionally.

Do's and Don'ts for Round Three

✓ **Do** compliment the skit and ask about the meaning behind something you learned. Be specific. Instead of just saying, "I loved the skit," say, "You really have a great voice!"

✓ **Do** take note of the photos of events like mixers, formals, and Greek Week displayed during the skit round. Ask specific questions: "What's going on in the photo?" or "Tell me about this event."

✓ **Do** maintain eye contact and continue to show enthusiasm for the process. It's almost over!

✓ **Do** start getting to know your fellow rushees—these are your potential new sisters.

✗ **Don't** talk just about yourself.

✗ **Don't** say things like, "I hate dressing up in formal wear." That gives the impression you aren't going to want to participate in sorority functions.

✗ **Don't** give the impression you won't have time for a sorority by talking about your full course load, your full-time job, the off-campus internship you hope to land, and your plans for a semester abroad.

✗ **Don't** act fake by laughing too hard, smiling constantly, or agreeing with absolutely everything someone says to you. If you're just not that into a particular sorority, that's all right. Just be nice and polite.

Conversation Starters for Round Three

1. "How long did you practice the skit?"

2. "Did someone in the sorority write the skit or is something you've done for years?"

3. "What was your favorite function last year?"

4. "Do you usually travel out of town for formals?"

5. "How long did it take to decorate for this round?"

Your turn! Come up with some questions for round three.

QUESTIONS FOR ROUND 3

1. _____

_____

2. _____

_____

3. _____

_____

4. _____

_____

5. _____

_____

SUCCESS STRATEGY This is your time. Is your mother or sister calling to ask if you're leaning toward their sororities? Remember, you're trying to find the best fit for you. Things may be getting stressful. Carve out some quiet time to allow yourself time to think and relax.

NOTES ON ROUND 3

BOTTOM LINE:

You will visit fewer sororities in this
round, and you'll have more time to
yourself. Use it wisely. Don't stress!
Remember to eat right and
get some exercise.

Round Four: Time to Choose (Preferential Day)

The last round, preferential day is an intimate, ceremonial, and often emotional day, as you and the sorority members make final choices. This round provides one final visit to the sororities that remain possibilities for you (up to three), to give you more time to ask more questions to find the best fit. This is the most serious round, where sororities will begin to reveal special significance of their colors or symbols.

Before this round, plan to spend some quiet time by yourself. Gather your thoughts on each sorority and think about where you truly feel you will find the best fit. Reflect on the charities, formal events, and other activities each sorority's members talked about and really consider which one will prepare you for a fun college experience and lifelong sisterhood. Keep your options and your mind open. Write down your thoughts about where you felt most comfortable.

When you arrive at each house, the sisters may be dressed alike, possibly in formal attire such as black dresses. They might be holding candles, or they may be lined up on the house's staircase. After welcoming you to the final round of rush, usually with a song, sisters will greet you for the last time as rushees.

Preferential day ceremonies differ at each house, but they'll be specific and moving. You might receive small token gifts with the Greek letters of the sorority on them. You may also receive handwritten notes from sorority members, telling you they enjoyed meeting you and that they feel you would be an asset to the house. These items all must stay in the house when you leave the preferential day round, as they are special, secret and sacred to each sorority.

You'll talk with several sorority members during this final round. It's important to be respectful and friendly at each house on preferential day. Do not assume that your first choice will be where you end up. Keep in mind this is the end of a long and often stressful week for the sorority members as well as potential new members.

Active sorority members may not express their preferences to prospective members during this round. No promises should be made. Potential new members should avoid blunt statements like, "I really hope I get a bid here." It's fine to express enthusiasm about your favorite. A more subtle statement such as, "I really feel at home here," or "I've enjoyed getting to know the sisters here," is better.

Do's and Don'ts for Round Four

✓ **Do** express your enthusiasm for your favorite sorority. When it comes time to make their final selections, sororities want to consider girls they know really want to join.

✓ **Do** pay attention to the other potential new members who are with you on preferential day. These girls could be your pledge class members. Choose the group where you feel the most comfortable.

✓ **Do** treat everyone with kindness and respect, and thank them for their hospitality during rush week.

✓ **Do** pay special attention when getting ready. Try to look your very best.

✗ **Don't** assume you're in, but don't assume you're going to be cut, either.

✗ **Don't** expect a guarantee like, "I'm sure you'll get a bid here." Active members are not allowed to make such statements.

✗ **Don't** say anything negative about anyone or anything. You want to end your rush experience on a positive note.

✗ **Don't** list just one sorority on your final bid card. This is called "suiciding" or "intentional single preference." It's very risky. Bids are determined by matching sororities' choices with rushees' preferences, but the sororities' choices take priority. Don't take a chance on not getting a bid at all. Suiciding can result in not making a match.

Conversation Starters for Round Four

1. "How did you choose this sorority?"

2. "What is the most special part of Greek life to you?"

3. "How has sorority life helped you?"

4. "What's your favorite memory of your pledge experience?"

5. "What are you looking for your new sisters to bring to the sorority?"

Your turn! Come up with a few questions or comments for round four.

QUESTIONS FOR ROUND 4

1. _____

_____

2. _____

_____

3. _____

_____

4. _____

_____

5. _____

_____

SUCCESS STRATEGY Reflect on why you started this process. You want to find a group of people that you can connect with during your college experience. List the sororities on your bid card where you can really see yourself as a member.

A final thought on rush: Just because you have gone through recruitment doesn't mean you must join a sorority. If you could not identify with any group, maybe sorority life is not for you. Really search your heart. If you don't feel connected to any group, tell your recruitment counselor and follow the proper procedure for leaving rush. It may seem painful, but it's the right thing to do.

NOTES ON ROUND 4

BOTTOM LINE:

This day is emotional, and you may have a strong sense of where you feel at home. Be true to yourself.

Bid Day

Your bid card is the list you will submit to the sororities, in your order of preference, indicating where you would like to receive an invitation. Prospective members sign their bid cards in a specific location, such as the student center on campus. After you have signed your card, try to relax! Watch TV, go for a run, or read a book. Try to get your mind off things for just a little while.

Remember to keep an open mind throughout the recruitment process, and carefully choose the sorority you feel is right for you. Don't feel pressured to choose a particular sorority because a friend did, or even because your mother or sister did. This is a time to choose what is best for you!

Sign your bid card with confidence and relax. You've done your best, met a ton of great people, and learned things that will help you in your future. Remember that participating in Greek life may be one of many things you will do in college—it will not be the only thing.

Bid Day and Beyond: Let's Get It Started!

With sorority members strict silence must be obeyed during rush, except during official recruitment events. Everything changes on Bid Day! Your recruitment counselor will advise you when and where bids are handed out. At this time you will learn which sorority has extended a bid, or an invitation to join. An invitation to join is not an obligation. Not everyone who receives a bid accepts it, and not everyone receives a bid.

As with the selection process, the bid matches are made by computer. Sororities have lists of everyone who visited on Preferential Day indicating their top choices. Likewise, your bid card will list your choices in order of preference. Say you named ABC sorority your first choice and EFG sorority your second choice. EFG sorority has ranked you at the very top of its list, but ABC sorority had many other girls ahead of you on its list. You could end up at EFG sorority.

If you didn't get your first choice, try not to feel disappointed.

The sorority members know their chapter better than you do, and they have a better sense of who would be a good fit. Often sororities are looking for different attributes at different times with different pledge classes.

Look at it this way: You were the first choice of the sorority you will be pledging!

Bid day is fun and exciting, the beginning of your sorority experience. When you accept the invitation to bid, your new sisters will greet you with hugs and gift bags containing items like a T-shirt, a key ring, or a notepad with your new sorority's letters. Then you and your new sisters will head to the house for a fun event like a cookout. Some sororities may hold a semi-formal ceremony, or you might watch movies or play games to get to know each other better.

The Pledge Process

The girls who accept bids become the sorority's pledge class, and are initiated into full membership several months after their pledge experience begins. As a member of the new pledge class, you'll be expected to attend regular chapter meetings, maintain a certain grade point average, and uphold the sorority's standards. The pledge process is a time of introduction. You will learn about your sorority and prove to the sisters that you are ready to make membership a priority in your life.

You'll be assigned a big sister, an active member who will serve as an advisor and special friend. In the weeks following bid day you will be required to attend regular chapter meetings. You may be required to take tests proving you have learned the history of your sorority and other facts discussed during chapter meetings.

As a pledge, you will meet all of the active members. You also get in on the fun! Within a few weeks you'll probably attend your first social functions—pledge formals are common, as are mixers with fraternities on campus. Soon it will be time to prepare for special events like Greek Week, sorority retreats, semi-formals, and formals.

You'll also get involved in your sorority's philanthropic endeavors. This will be a busy time. Classes will have started, and you'll have to juggle your academic requirements with chapter obligations and social functions.

Sororities with houses on campus usually have house cooks and meal plans; those that do not have houses may have designated areas in the dining hall where pledges and members sit together at meals. Take the opportunity to sit with different people at meals, rather than falling into the habit of eating with the same group each time.

Your Initiation

At the end of your pledge process you'll participate in an initiation ceremony. Your sorority's initiation is a most special time. You will understand the true meaning of your sorority and the traditions it holds sacred. The secrets and traditions that are revealed to you during initiation are to be held in the highest confidence. At initiation you will become a true sorority sister. You must now uphold the standards and good reputation of your sorority because you are a lifelong member of this very special group of women.

It is great knowing that you have the support of your sorority as you experience college and all of its excitement.

Wear your Greek letters proudly—you've earned them.

FAQs of Recruitment/Rush

Q: I've heard certain sororities have reputations. Should that guide my decision?

A: No! Sororities are made up of diverse girls with different interests. Find the one that's your best fit. Don't let preconceived notions influence you.

Q: If I am a legacy, does that ensure a bid?

A: No. Legacy status will get you a closer look but it's no guarantee.

Q: When and where do I send photos of myself?

A: Photos are not generally included with registration materials, but do include a photo in each rec package.

Q: Do I have to go to all the parties?

A: Yes. Recruitment is designed to help you learn about all aspects of Greek life. Participate fully; otherwise, you're just cheating yourself. At some schools, you will be dropped from recruitment if you do not attend all parties.

Q: Do sororities haze?

A: Hazing, which is when someone is forced to do something physically or emotionally harmful, is strictly forbidden by sororities and colleges.

Q: How do I find out about costs?

A: Some college Web sites will include estimates of the cost of Greek life. If not, contact the Panhellenic office at your school.

Q: How do sororities decide who to invite back to their parties?

A: The members vote after each round to decide which girls to invite back. The sororities' choices and rushees' choices are run through a computer by Panhellenic officials, generating the next list of recruitment invitees.

Q: If I go through recruitment, do I have to join?

A: No. You are not obligated to accept a bid.

Q: What happens if I don't accept a bid?

A: Think very carefully before deciding not to accept a bid. If you do, you won't be able to join a sorority until the next recruitment process (usually a year later).

Q: How do I choose a sorority?

A: Find the group whose members you truly connect with, and a place where you feel at home. Don't feel like you must select a sorority because your mother was a member, or because your roommate is leaning toward it. Choose the place where you really see yourself.

BOTTOM LINE:

The process you've just completed is valuable! You've learned to prepare your resume, network with people who can help you achieve your goals, introduce yourself, and carry on conversations. You've learned to examine choices and deal with disappointment, and you've made lots of new friends.

No matter how recruitment turned out, congratulations are in order!

A Day to Remember!

On _____ I got a bid from _____

My Big Sister is _____

My sorority's colors are _____

The official jewel is _____

The official flower is _____

Some notes from bid day to cherish always!

NOTES ON BID DAY

_____

_____

_____

_____

_____

_____

_____

_____

_____

_____

_____

_____

CHAPTER SIX

A Day in the Life:

Recruitment from Both Sides

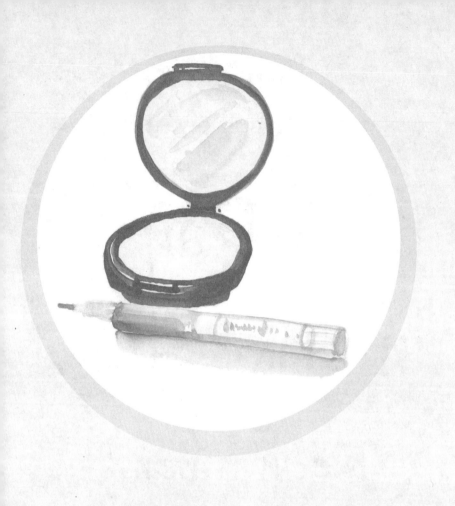

A Day in the Life: Recruitment from Both Sides

We talked to current and alumnae sorority members
to get the views of what your day might be like as a rushee—
and what the sorority members' day is like during this process.
Here's a dramatized account, based on
various members' experiences.

The rushee

Sarah attends a college where recruitment is held in the fall,
prior to the start of classes. She wants to join a sorority to meet
new people. Girls from her high school have told her about all the
fun sorority life offers.

Sarah has kept a close eye on all materials her school sent
her over the summer, and she filled out her recruitment registration
form on-line. Her mother, older sisters, and some family friends
who were in sororities have sent in letters of recommendation that
highlight her good character and the value she would bring to a
sorority.

On the first day of rush, she wakes up early (hopefully she
was able to get some sleep the night before) and hops in the shower.
Our girl is smart enough to head straight for the bathroom in her
dorm before every other girl on the hall is in there trying to shower.

Back in her room, Sarah has her clothes pressed and ready
to go. Round One is fairly casual at her school, so she's deciding
whether to wear a flower-print skirt or cotton capris with a

sleeveless cotton top. She chooses the skirt, and a cute pair of flip-flops decorated with ribbon. Of course, Sarah has worn the shoes before, so they are comfortable. She knows not to wear brand-new shoes that could give her blisters and make it difficult and painful to walk to the different houses.

She ties her hair back into a low, simple ponytail and secures it with a ribbon that goes with her outfit. She wants to look casual and comfortable, but still neat and put together. She applies a little blush and eye shadow and shimmery lip gloss—just enough to give a nice, healthy glow. She knows she'll be walking a lot and visiting many houses. She doesn't want fussy makeup that's going to have to be touched up every twenty minutes.

At the designated time, Sarah meets with her recruitment counselor and fellow rushees for the beginning of round one. At Sarah's school, potential new members walk from house to house (but at others, rushees may travel by bus to the various sororities).

At each house, the sisters break into a spirited song to welcome the girls. Their voices are so incredibly loud that the windows seem to be rattling! After the song ends, the prospective members are invited in. A sorority member greets Sarah at each house and introduces herself. Sarah spends a few minutes talking with two or three members at each house. She knows the questions will begin to sound the same, but Sarah finds ways to make the conversations interesting.

"Which dorm do you live in?" one sister asks her.

"Smith Dorm," Sarah answers. "I love the location, since it's near the track. I ran cross-country in high school."

The member asks about Sarah's experience on the cross-country team. The best part, Sarah says, "was when my team volunteered to work with Special Olympics athletes." Pretty soon it's time to move on——but Sarah made the most of her brief conversation. Later, when members are trying to put names with faces, they'll probably recall tons of girls who said they lived in Smith Dorm. Sarah, who managed to take a routine question and reveal an interesting fact about herself, will stand out.

Throughout the day, including during the lunch break, Sarah gets to know her fellow rushees, including her roommate, a little better. She asks where they're from, shares a little about herself, and wishes everyone good luck. At the end of her first day, Sarah is worn out! The day began at eight in the morning and lasted until nearly four in the afternoon, with about fifteen to twenty minutes at each house. Sarah takes a long shower and goes to bed early. Even if she wasn't exhausted, she knows this is not the time to be partying all night.

On the second and third days, Sarah visits fewer houses, as she and the sororities are all making their choices. She is a little disappointed that a house she really liked cuts her after the first round, but she keeps a positive attitude and an open mind. Sarah is looking for two or three sororities where she feels at home. The second and third rounds start later in the day but each visit lasts longer than visits in the first round, between thirty and forty-five minutes. During round two, the house tour, Sarah asks about the interesting architectural features of the houses and mentions she once volunteered during her hometown's tour of historic homes. During skit day, when sisters have decorated the house with photos of themselves at various sorority functions, Sarah asks about the events. She shows sincere and genuine interest as the members talk about what's going on in the photos. The days are not as long as the first day, when potential new members visited all of the houses on campus, but they're still tiring.

After each round Sarah comes back to her room and spends some quiet time mentally reviewing the day. Sarah makes some notes about her impression of each house and the girls she met. Later these notes will help as she narrows her choices. She and her roommate discuss each round. Her roommate didn't get invited back to her favorite chapter after the first round, and Sarah encourages her to stick with it and keep an open mind.

On philanthropy day, Sarah enjoys wearing shorts and the rush T-shirt with tennis shoes. The girls all decorate teddy bears that will be donated to children who have gone through a fire or other disaster. Sarah has a good time talking to the active members and her fellow rushees about the smiles they'll put on the children's faces.

During the later rounds Sarah wears dressier outfits and a little more makeup. She wears her hair long. (Naturally, she had gotten a haircut and highlights a couple of weeks before recruitment began.) She chooses a longer skirt with sandals and a dressy top for the second round and a sleeveless linen dress she would wear to church for the third. She wore comfortable sandals the first couple of days, then foolishly wore a new pair of mules to skit day, even thought she knew better. Her feet ache and she has ended the day with a terrible blister. She hopes the sisters didn't see her limping in pain as she left the final house. Luckily she brought Band-Aids with her.

Sarah overhears some of the potential new members gossiping about others in the recruitment process, criticizing some of the sorority houses, and complaining about how lame some of the songs were. Sarah knows the sorority members have worked hard to get ready for rush and does not participate in the conversation. Likewise, when fellow rushees ask if she's decided which sorority she wants to join, she is polite but doesn't say anything negative about any sorority or rush itself.

"I haven't made up my mind yet. I'm having fun getting to know more about the houses and I hope I find a great match," she says to one of her fellow prospects. "I hope you do, too."

At the end of each day during the process, Sarah's recruitment counselor collects the choices of each girl in her group, and returns from the Panhellenic office with the list of sororities everyone will visit the next day. The night before the preferential round, the counselor brings Sarah the list of the two houses that have invited her back for a final visit. Sarah's excited because those two chapters are ones where she felt a strong connection.

She's aware that some rushees were invited back to more chapters for the preferential round, and some were only given one choice.

She decides to take a run and think about all the girls she has met and which sorority truly seems like the best fit for her.

The night before the final round of recruitment, things are very emotional on her hall. She has seen some girls crying. Sarah runs into a group of girls talking in hushed voices in the hall of her dorm. Apparently one girl in their rush group has dropped out and is very upset.

"She was a legacy and she got cut," one of the girls says sympathetically.

Sarah recalls this girl told everyone she was going to pledge the YZ sorority because her sister had been in that sorority. She didn't bother getting recommendations for any other sorority and acted disinterested and bored at some of the other houses. To Sarah, she never seemed open to any sorority except the one where she had legacy status. She boxed herself in and couldn't deal when it didn't work out her way, Sarah figures.

"I hope she has someone to talk to at home," Sarah tells the group. She is glad she has kept an open mind throughout the recruitment process and did not have her heart set on any one house. She feels sorry for the girl who didn't seem emotionally prepared for the possibility she would not get her first choice.

On preferential day, dress at Sarah's school is very specific. All potential new sorority members were told to wear simple black dresses to this round. The event starts in the early afternoon and girls spend about an hour at each chapter. Sisters in formal attire at each sorority greet them. During the preferential round, Sarah talks with girls at the two sororities she has grown to really like during recruitment. This will be a difficult decision! As she is leaving the last party, she talks with the very first girl she met in round one. It was the member who had asked which dorm she lived in. Sarah's response, which led to a conversation about her cross-country experience and how much she enjoyed working with Special Olympics events, remained in that member's mind all throughout recruitment. She makes a special point to talk with Sarah during this final round, and tells her what a great addition she would make to the house.

Sarah has decided she really wants to go Greek. That night, she completes her bid card. By this time Sarah is convinced she knows which sorority she wants to join, and she lists it first. Since she knows that listing only one choice is risky, she lists the other chapter second, and looks forward to participating in Greek life.

After a near-sleepless night, Sarah reports to the student center, where bid day is held. Sarah is thrilled to learn she will be pledging her first choice! Her roommate got a bid from a sorority that wasn't her first choice but where she met some really great girls during the process.

Sarah and the other newest members rush to greet their new sisters. Sarah is welcomed to her new Greek home by the member who made her feel so special during the last preferential round visit. That girl is Beth. Here's her side of the story.

The recruiter

So what's Beth been going through this week?

Well, to be honest, she's been getting ready for recruitment for months. A sophomore now, Beth was in Sarah's shoes just a year ago. Although rush was hard, she loves her sorority, and takes her responsibility to help pick the best pledges very seriously. She knows how stressful recruitment can be for rushees. Now she's about to find out what it's like on the other side.

The sorority's rush chairman started getting the members in gear before the spring semester ended. Members got recruitment-week assignments. They met over the summer to work on songs, skits, and cheers. They worked for hours making signs to welcome the potential new members, and put photos of past sorority events on display for skit day. Before returning to school all the sisters hit the salons to get manicures and highlights.

By the time recruitment started, Beth and her sorority sisters have been back at school for at least a couple of days. They're spending their time getting ready for recruitment. Everyone wants to make a great first impression.

Round one begins. The first recruitment party starts at nine in the morning. Prospective members were meeting with their recruitment counselors at eight, but the sororities' members have been up for hours by that time, working on last-minute decorating and getting everything ready to meet the first round of rushees. Beth finds her place in the front of the line. Her heart beats a mile a minute as she and her sorority sisters start singing. The sorority members are as nervous as the rushees! Beth knows how brutally nerve-wracking rush can be on the other side, but didn't realize how jittery she would feel as a member. To keep their energy up the girls sing at the top of their lungs. They're excited to meet all the new rushees. After the song ends they file outside and invite the girls inside.

Beth talks to two or three girls for a few minutes each during each party this first day. She's an outgoing girl who loves to talk, but pretty soon conversations get repetitive. If Beth has to ask one more girl what her major is, she may scream. But she knows she is part of her sorority's first impression on potential new sisters and does her best to keep conversations moving along.

Beth, like her sisters, has been assigned a certain number of girls to meet and talk to. She feels pressure to remember everything she can about these girls, as she will be reporting back to the entire group about them later.

After each group departs, Beth and her sisters have just a few minutes to jot down some notes about each girl they talked with. After the first party, Beth makes a note about a girl named Sarah.

As the next party nears, the sisters rush around to straighten up and get themselves ready before the second group arrives and it all starts again.

Finally the last party ends, but the day has really just begun for the sorority sisters. Now they must begin to tax their weary brains to remember something about each of the hundreds of girls they have met. The sisters, who ate a quick lunch provided by some of the Rush Moms who are in town to assist during the recruitment process, take a break for dinner. Then it's time to get to work.

Some cuts are easy. The girls who yawned the entire time and kept looking at their watches, the ones whose resumes and applications were full of misspelled words: goodbye. There was one girl who seemed to be playing a practical joke on someone (maybe herself) by showing up in a ripped tank top and cut-off shorts. Was she serious? Who knows? She won't be back.

It's a little more difficult to weed through the girls who all seemed nice enough but didn't really stand out. Yes, their resumes and recommendations looked good, but almost everyone's paperwork looks good. Because there are only so many slots, many girls who would probably be great additions to the house must be let go. It's simply a matter of numbers.

It's a little early for sisters to start really pulling for girls, but Beth speaks up when Sarah's name is called. "I met her and she was really awesome," Beth says. "She was fun to talk to. I asked her which dorm she lived in and she ended up telling me about how she worked with Special Olympics."

By the time all the cuts are made, it's well past midnight, and the sisters have just a few hours before they have to get up and start the second day. During the second and third rounds, Beth continues to get up very early and stay up very late.

Although most of the prospects seem to be enjoying recruitment, Beth is shocked by a few inappropriate remarks. One girl asks what kind of cars the sorority sisters drive – she's clearly just interested in the chapter with the wealthiest members. Another spends more time admiring herself in the mirror than anything else. One girl actually asks, "Are we about done? The next house I'm going to is the one I really like."

These girls, of course, aren't doing themselves any favors. But they do make it easier on the sisters when it comes time to select the prospects who will be invited back. They're the first names on the chopping block.

The nights get later and longer as recruitment progresses. By this time many of Beth's sorority sisters have certain girls they're pushing. Girls who are legacies must be invited back to a certain number of rounds, but it's become clear that some of these girls have no interest in the sorority. It seems like they're only there because their mother or sister has talked them into it, and they've been acting like they're doing everyone a big favor by just showing up. Well, thanks but no thanks, the sisters ultimately decide in a few cases, and the dreaded legacy cut has been made. No member wants to cut a legacy, but sometimes it has to be done.

Beth takes her responsibilities seriously and knows her sisters are counting on her to give an accurate representation of each of the girls she has been assigned.

She is pleased that a number of her sisters apparently think as highly of Sarah as she does. Other girls she liked, however, are getting cut. One girl Beth and some of the others thought would be an asset to the sorority is being blackballed by a senior member. Oops! It turns out the girl went to a prom with this member's ex-boyfriend three years ago. Obviously the rushee had no way of knowing this, but the senior is using her influence. The girl will not be invited back, no matter how unfair it seems. Beth resists the temptation to argue, knowing that the best thing for the sorority as a whole is to invite back rushees everyone likes.

The night before the preferential round, Beth and her sorority sisters are about to drop. They have gotten up early and stayed up late every night. There's been no going out during this time. No one can wear sorority letters around campus, and strict silence must be obeyed. It's a tiring process but one Beth knows will be worth it. At the end of the week, her sorority will have a group of great new girls to welcome!

For the first three rounds of recruitment, Beth and her sorority sisters have had specific outfits to wear. One day it was shorts with T-shirts designed just for rush.` Another day everyone wore skirts and tops in specified colors. For preferential day, the sisters all wear white dresses to symbolize their pure hearts. They line up on the staircase, each holding a glowing candle, and sing one of their sorority's special anthems as the groups enter the house. Afterward, sisters spend time talking about girls they have gotten to know during the week. They talk about what the sorority experience has meant to them, and how they feel the new girls would enhance the chapter. Beth is pleased to get a chance to talk with Sarah during the last pref round party.

After the final group has gone, the night seems to go on forever. The girls invited to the pref round are ranked in order of the sorority's preference. The sorority submits its list to Panhellenic officials who run everything through a computer. The matches are made electronically, with rushees' choices and sororities' choices aligned. It's a long and sleepless night as sisters wonder who will become the newest pledge class.

Finally, bid day arrives and matches are announced. Beth is excited that Sarah is among the girls who will be joining her sorority! Sisters greet their new pledges with gifts of T-shirts, key chains, and note cards with the Greek letters of the sorority on them. They all head back to the house for a cookout, followed by games to get to know everyone better. It's time for everyone to relax, at last.

Although our examples are hypothetical, the lessons for you are real:

- The first girl you meet could be the one who fights hardest to keep you, so make the most of your time with everyone.
- The recruitment experience can be brutal on the rushee, but it's also tough on the sorority member.
- Stick with it, and keep an open mind—it will be worth it in the end.

Thoughts from some who have been there

"Rushees are not competing against each other for the best sorority – the sororities are competing against each other for the best girls. The pledges are the prize." *– Active sophomore member*

"Don't let the stereotypes rule you: Certain houses get reputations: the wealthy house, the house with all the beauty queens, the athletic types. Gauge for yourself when you're going through it. Don't let stereotypes hold you back." *– Recent graduate*

"There's no one 'right' type for sororities. The girls you will meet come from all sorts of backgrounds. It's a good cross-section." *– Senior member*

"Go in without expectations, be yourself, be real, don't try too hard. Be classy. Get to know people. Be yourself." *– Sorority alumna*

"After rush you'll never be uncomfortable in a crowd of strangers again." *– Recent graduate*

CHAPTER SEVEN

Fashion Sense —

The Whole Package

Fashion Sense—
The Whole Package

At all the events during the recruitment process, it's important to put your best self forward, and feel comfortable and confident. Your goal is to look polished and appropriate throughout the entire recruitment process.

The first step is to look for guidelines in your recruitment booklet or advice on what to wear on your school's Web site. Lots of college Web sites show pictures of girls in outfits suitable for each round on the Greek pages of their sites. If not, there might be photos of past recruitments where girls are shown in various looks from casual to formal for different rounds of rush. Pay attention to those cues. Check www.sororityguide.com for more suggestions.

Talk to girls you know who have participated in rush at the school you'll be attending, and ask for tips on what to wear. If you're going through deferred recruitment, take a look around campus before rush begins. Pay attention to what girls are wearing and get with it.

Rush week isn't the time for a daring new haircut or ultra-trendy look. Your goal is to look appropriate and fit in, not try to copy the pages of a fashion magazine in search of a style that doesn't really suit you. If you will be doing a lot of walking, wear comfy shoes, put your nice shoes in a bag, and change just before you go inside the party. It's hard to put your best foot forward if it's blistered. Repeat after us: No New Shoes!

Keep in mind that the skirt that looks so hot when you are standing up may be a fashion nightmare if you have to sit. Depending on how the houses or chapter rooms are set up, you might be sitting on the floor for parts of each party. You want the sisters to remember your great smile and sparkling personality, not what's under your skirt.

Different regions of the country have different fashion senses, so take some time to get familiar with the way girls at your school dress. This is especially important if you grew up in one area of the country and plan to attend college in another. Say you're from the North, where sorority recruitment functions might call for business attire, but you're going to school in the South, where linen dresses are the norm. (Show up in a dark blue suit in the summertime in Birmingham, and people might wonder if you've just come from a funeral. Wear a sundress to a school in Boston, and they could think you're a tourist.) Similarly, shorts and flip-flops may be just fine on some campuses but totally inappropriate on others.

Rush week is the time for you to get to know your potential new sisters, and for them to get to know you. Believe us—you'll feel most comfortable if the focus is your accomplishments or wonderful personality, not your wardrobe. Think carefully before wearing your toe ring or nose stud. These may be true expressions of your style, but remember, the girls you're going to be meeting must make quick decisions based on first impressions.

At most every school during recruitment, the attire starts out more casual and gradually becomes more dressy as the process progresses. Many campuses have very specific requirements for the final found of recruitment. Your recruitment counselor is there to help; when in doubt, ask!

SUCCESS STRATEGIES to get you started

- Get everything ready to go the night before each round. Take your clothes to the dry cleaners ahead of time. That way they'll also be perfectly pressed, and your dry cleaner can make simple repairs, if needed. The morning you want to wear a top is a bad time to notice a stain or realize you're missing a button.

- Not everything has to be brand-new (you definitely don't want to wear brand-new shoes). Choose pieces you feel great in and that you know will look great for hours. Try on everything ahead of time. Sit down in your outfits and walk around in new shoes.

Check yourself out from every angle in a full-length mirror.

Stylishly simple is always best. Don't wear anything that's super trendy, but don't dress like your mother, either. Revealing, tight, and clingy are always no-nos.

Find things that express your own personal style. This isn't the time to go retro if you're just not into that look. You're not going to pull off a new style that doesn't really suit you. Wear what you know looks awesome on you—not necessarily something you saw on the latest reality show.

Invest in a good haircut, highlights, and a manicure. Nothing dramatic. Shape your eyebrows, but don't over pluck.

It's time to take off your high school class ring.

What to wear to each round: A sample of possibilities

Round One: Ice-Water Tea or Open House

Polished and appropriate is the way to go. In warm climates, that means a sundress, skirt, or capris with a cute top. If shorts are appropriate at your school, pair them with nice sandals to dress them up a bit.

Several girls we talked to said flip-flops are just fine for this round, but not the type you wear in the shower. Think cute and stylish ones that are dressy-casual.

At campuses where rush is held in cooler climates, a skirt or slacks with a sweater set would be a good choice. Choose fashionable yet comfortable shoes that complement your outfit. If your campus calls for business attire, this is a business-casual round.

Fashion Do's and Don'ts for Round One

✓ **Do** shop early in the season so you'll have the best selection of clothes.

✓ **Do** have more outfits than you need in case you need to make a change. You'll also fee less stressed if you have more than one option each day. Tragedy does strike (in the form of spilled Diet Cokes, for example).

✓ **Do** carry a tote or hand bag with your "must-have" items (umbrella, breath mints, walking shoes, and lip gloss). Your rush counselor will watch your bags during the party.

✗ **Don't** be afraid to wear inexpensive pieces, but make sure they're well tailored and aren't obvious knockoffs of well-known designers.

✗ **Don't** let your clothes overtake you. Let your personality shine.

Round Two: The House Tour or Philanthropy Day

Philanthropy day is usually more casual. You might be provided a T-shirt to wear. Pair it with shorts, capris, or a khaki skirt, or wear a great pair of designer jeans if they're acceptable on your campus.

Wear basic jewelry that goes with your outfit. Express your personal style without going overboard. It is okay to express your fashion sense by wearing the latest trends.

If business wear is called for, a less casual outfit—but not quite a business suit—would be appropriate.

Fashion Do's and Don'ts for Round Two

✓ **Do** make sure your skirts and shorts are the appropriate length. We suggest no shorter than mid-thigh.

✓ **Do** look polished, even in casual clothes.

✗ **Don't** show up with a fussy manicure. French manicures, pale colors, or clear nails are best.

✗ **Don't** wear too much makeup.

Round Three: Skit Day

Attire becomes more formal. Choose a dress you might wear to a wedding, church, or synagogue—not a cocktail dress, but definitely more dressy than casual. A patterned skirt and blouse or a conservative dress in the latest style would look great.

Fashion Do's and Don'ts for Round Three

✓ **Do** remember to express your own style. Accessorize your outfit. Feel confident in the clothes you've chosen for recruitment.

✓ **Do** have your clothes pressed, laid out, and ready to go the night before you'll be wearing them.

✗ **Don't** worry about designer labels or the cost of an outfit, as long as you look put together and polished.

✗ **Don't** choose outfits that wrinkle easily. The days will be long and action packed; you don't want to look messy at the end of the day.

Round Four: Preferential Day

Dress can be very specific on the last day of rush, when girls and sororities have one final chance to get to know each other. With just a few parties to attend, you'll have more time to get ready and look your personal best.

Rush materials from your school and the Greek page on the Web site will give guidance about what to wear and tell you if specific colors are suggested for this round. On some campuses the girls wear white dresses, on others they wear black dresses. Business suits are suitable for this round in some regions, while other campuses call for nonspecific formal attire on preferential day. At some schools, this is a dress you'd wear to a wedding. At others, it's a dress you would wear to a dressy nighttime event. Pay attention, especially to pictures! Be sure to dress appropriately.

Fashion Do's and Don'ts for Preferential Day

✓ **Do** look your very best.

✓ **Do** give yourself plenty of time to get ready.

✗ **Don't** wear anything short, clingy, or revealing.

✗ **Don't** overstyle yourself.

Bid Day

This varies from campus to campus, with some calling for very casual outfits (including a T-shirt with the Greek letters of your new sorority) and others calling for more formal attire like pure white dresses or cocktail dresses. Your new sisters want this day to be special for you! They might even help you choose what to wear.

Fashion Do's and Don'ts for Bid Day

✓ **Do** be glad you've found your Greek home!

✓ **Do** follow the dress code at your campus.

✗ **Don't** regret a minute of your recruitment process!

More What-to-Wear Resources

▪ Campus Web sites offer helpful, specific advice about all things related to recruitment, including what to wear. The Arizona State University Web site (www.asu.edu), for example, includes photos of girls in sample outfits for each round. The suggested clothes at ASU range from capris and casual tops to skirts and sandals to dresses you'd wear to a special event.

▪ Campus newspapers and their Web sites are also a great source of information. We found a very helpful and well-written article on the Web site for the *Daily Mississippian*, the student newspaper at the University of Mississippi (www.thedmonline.

com). The article advised starting in khaki shorts and tennis shoes, then progressing to more formal attire, ending up with dresses appropriate for a banquet. It also advised wearing comfy shoes when trekking from house to house, and changing into your dressier (less comfortable) shoes right before going in.

Knowing what NOT to wear is just as important as knowing what to wear. We like the Greek page on the Web site for California State University-Chico (www.chicogreeks.com), because it gives do's and don'ts. Examples of things to leave behind: too-short shorts and pantyhose and dress shoes.

Be sure to check your school's Web site for specifics to your campus. Pantyhose may be out in California, but the Appalachian State University Web site (www.appstate.edu) recommends hose and heels for the preferential round.

Be aware of regional differences in clothing. The Greek page on the University of Chicago's Web site (greekcouncil.uchicago.edu) spells out what to wear for each round of rush. Among the recommendations are business-casual dress for philanthropy day, pantsuits for skit day, and cocktail dresses for the preferential round and bid day.

BOTTOM LINE:

Project a look that is well put together and appropriate for your school. Be sure to wear your best accessory, your smile. Step forward with style and confidence.

CHAPTER EIGHT

The Balancing Act:

Keeping an Open Mind, Avoiding Disappointment

The Balancing Act: Keeping an Open mind, Avoiding Disappointment

You and a friend hit the mall. You are going to die if you don't get this one particular item. Maybe it's a hot top you saw in a magazine or a cute skirt a friend has. You decide you will not leave the mall without it, even if you have to rip it off a mannequin. You spend the day tearing through every rack at every store. No luck. The first place has just sold the last one. The second place doesn't have your size. The third place doesn't carry it at all. Before long you are seriously hating life.

Meanwhile, your friend who accompanied you on this shopping trip didn't have a particular item in mind. She just knew she wanted—something that fit well and made her feel great. Because she didn't have her heart set on one particular thing, she kept an open mind and tried lots of looks before finding the perfect outfit.

As you leave, your friend is pumped about her purchases. Everything looks amazing on her. You, on the other hand, are wearing nothing new but an irritated expression. You were so into that one item that you didn't even notice tons of awesome buys you could have gotten.

Don't let your search for a sorority end up like this shopping trip! Keep an open mind and set out to find a good fit, just like your friend. "The more attached, the more you absolutely have to have it, the more you limit projecting your best self. You become narrow-minded," says stress-management expert Donna Brooks.

"The more we want something, the more wrapped up we get around it, the more we

get tight and obsessive. These are the very things that keep our natural poise and grace from showing."

The less you stress about the recruitment process, the more likely you are to be pleased with the result, says Brooks, who leads seminars on poise and body image. "When you want something badly, the temptation is to obsess over it," she says. "Those repetitive thoughts often cause stress, worry, and futile attempts to control all aspects of the outcome. By all means know what you want and imagine getting it, but also let go and just have fun. That cultivates poise."

Tools to Keep Your Cool

By following a few stress-management tips during recruitment, you'll find you enjoy the process and the result a lot more. Here are our recommendations:

- Exercise. It's the best thing you can do to eliminate anxiety.

- Visualize success! You've heard of Olympic athletes who actually see themselves wearing the gold medal long before the games begin. Use this strategy.

- Focus on something else to give yourself a mental break every once in a while during rush. If you find your mind is racing with thoughts about the next round or you're feeling really stressed about bid day, organize your dorm room (which you probably need to do anyway). Download some iTunes and burn yourself a relaxing CD, or head for the student center to see what's up.

- Eat right. If you're jumpy anyway, sugary snacks or a steady stream of high-octane cappuccinos aren't going to help. Choose healthy snacks and drink plenty of water.

- Get plenty of sleep. If you can't sleep, at least try to rest. This isn't the time for parties or multi-night sleep-overs. You can't put your best foot forward if you're too tired to lift it.

Dealing with Disappointment

As college enrollments increase and more girls go through the recruitment process competing for a limited number of membership slots, disappointment is bound to occur. There may be small disappointments along the way, such as not getting invited back to a sorority you really liked. If you don't get a bid to your first choice, or rush doesn't end your way, it's not the end of the world. Every year, for whatever reason, there are lots of girls who just don't find a fit during recruitment. It happens. Life goes on. At some schools up to twenty-five percent of the girls who go through rush don't end up joining a sorority.

Dr. Mark R. Leary, professor and chair in the Department of Psychology at Wake Forest University, is a nationally recognized expert on social psychology, including anxiety and social acceptance. Author of more than one hundred scholarly articles, his books include *Self-Presentation: Impression Management and Interpersonal Behavior* (1995), *Social Anxiety* (1995), and *Interpersonal Rejection* (2001).

"Sorority rush is a pressure cooker for social anxiety,"

Leary says. "It's perfectly natural and, in fact, we'd have to wonder about a woman who was not socially anxious during the process." What's more, we're genetically programmed to get antsy in certain social situations. "Human beings have evolved as a social species with an exceptionally strong need for social acceptance," Leary says, noting that for our earliest ancestors, survival literally depended on being accepted by others.

"Part of successfully navigating the rush process is to understand that we are inherently programmed to take social acceptance and rejection very seriously,"

Leary says. Our natural inclination when feeling anxious is to clam up and become reticent—just the opposite of what potential new members ought to do during the recruitment process. Better to adopt the strategy Leary calls being "innocuously sociable—pleasant, agreeable, attentive, and engaged without saying any more than one has to."

If rush results in disappointment for whatever reason, it's important to put things in perspective. "The sorority's decision is the response of a relatively small number of other women in one organization on one campus, and thus says virtually nothing about [one's] social worth, attractiveness, or desirability to other people," Leary says. "Beware of ruminating oneself into misery. Rush is stressful, and rejection, should it occur, is very hurtful." Some people make things worse by mentally obsessing about the process, particularly about how things might go wrong.

The good news is, a temporary disappointment can ultimately result in positive emotional growth. "If a person who is rejected by a group can practice self-compassion rather than being self-critical, a great deal of personal growth can occur," Leary says. "People do bounce back." Don't do anything rash. Bouncing back can take time, and disappointment puts a damper on decision-making skills.

Dr. Jean Twenge, an assistant professor at San Diego State University's Department of Psychology, has conducted research on social acceptance. Her research has found:

- IQ scores actually go down after rejection. "You do not want to be making big life decisions when you are sad after being socially rejected," she says. "You're not thinking straight." Before you consider rejecting a bid from a sorority because it wasn't your first choice, dropping out of rush because your favorite house cut you after the first round, or something as drastic as leaving school because of a disappointing rush experience, give yourself time to settle down. A hasty decision made right after a social disappointment is bound to be one you'll regret.

- Comfort food is key. People in her research study groups eat treats like cookies after they've been rejected in carefully controlled experiments. ("Before you end up eating the whole carton of ice cream, put down the spoon," Twenge advises.)

Letdowns lead to putting off. People who have been rejected tend to procrastinate.

You really will get over it. "Right after something happens, it feels awful, like it's never going to go away," Twenge says. "It seems people have a fairly natural and automatic social resilience after rejection. A sorority rejection is going to hurt, but you'll recover. It won't hurt as long as you might think."

No matter what happens, the end result can be positive

Dr. Lyndon Waugh is a child psychiatrist who has seen many college students. He is also the author of *Tired of Yelling: Teaching Our Children to Resolve Conflict* (Longstreet, 1999). And he was a rush chairman his senior year at Dartmouth, so he's familiar with Greek life.

"I would recommend embracing the rush process with the attitude of being relaxed, open," he advises.

"A lot of times when social things don't work out, it's because people are trying too hard."

He suggests potential new members adopt a simple attitude: "I'm going to relax, be myself, tell the truth, not try to overly impress." If recruitment works out, great! But if not, it's important to remember: "I'm not going to base my whole self esteem on whether a certain group of people like me."

Either way, sorority life isn't all there is to college. "There's academics, there's friends you meet elsewhere, there's other activities and clubs, and there's dating," Waugh says. "Joining a sorority can be a part of it, but it's not the be-all, end-all."

Tips from Dr. Waugh:

- If you are friendly, authentic, and curious, and listen well, then you will likely be accepted by those who are more truly compatible.

- If recruitment doesn't result in a match for you, don't presume you know other people's minds regarding why you didn't get accepted. It could be numbers, jealousy, or one or two people.

- Don't act cocky or like you're the prize catch. If things don't go your way, you're likely to feel especially foolish—or be inappropriately defensive.

- Remember: You're so much more than this one thing.

If Recruitment Doesn't End Your Way

We've said it over and over, but it bears repeating. Not everyone is going to get a bid at her first-choice sorority, and some girls end the recruitment process without getting a bid at all.

Often it is simply a matter of numbers. Surging college enrollments mean there are more girls than ever competing for a limited number of spots. Listing just one sorority on your preferential card can leave you without a spot if you weren't ranked high enough by that sorority. We've also heard of cases where computer glitches were to blame.

In some cases, an unsuccessful recruitment experience can be a time for self-reflection. "If you went through the rush process bragging about how cool you are, how many guys you dated, how much money you have," Dr. Lyndon Waugh says, "it shouldn't be a shock if things somehow don't go your way. The good news is, this can still be a positive opportunity."

"A lot of times rejection can be lesson-teaching,"

Waugh says. "Then you can learn from your mistakes, if you clearly made some. If not, you learn to put such situations into perspective."

So if recruitment ends and you're not happy for whatever reason, take some time to reflect on the experience. Perhaps you'll want to participate in recruitment again in the future (you'll be even more prepared). If you felt you got lost among the numbers, use your time to get to know girls in class and on campus. You may them see at recruitment events in the future.

If your soul-searching reveals you acted a little too "all that," this is a good time to get real. Whether you rush again in the future or participate in other social and sports opportunities on campus, your personality check-up will leave you better prepared for all life has in store for you.

Joining a sorority may be one thing you do during college, but it's not the only thing. Sorority membership may be what you do, but it's not who you are. It's important to stay balanced and give yourself a break.

It may be tempting to mope and mourn, and it's okay to give yourself some down time. But don't stay down for long. Get involved in clubs or activities on your campus. Check out volunteer opportunities. Consider a part-time job. Just get busy! College is such a short and special time in your life. Don't waste time looking back.

BOTTOM LINE:

"As much as possible, whatever happens, tell yourself: nothing ventured, nothing gained. If you win, it's terrific, if you lose, it's not that big of a deal."

– Dr. Lyndon Waugh

CHAPTER NINE

Legacies:

A Tale of Two Sisters

Legacies:
A Tale of Two Sisters

There's really no nice way to say this, so here goes. Legacies aren't all that. Yes, the sororities are required to keep legacies around for a certain number of rounds, but they're not going to give you a bid just because your mother, sister, or grandmother was in a sorority.

Don't feel bad. We're talking numbers here. College enrollments have gone through the roof since your mother or grandmothers were in school. If you've grown up hearing about all the terrific times your grandmother, sister, or mother had in her sorority you may start rush believing there's only one place you want to be. However, the number of girls on campus in many cases far exceeds the number of open slots. Sometimes there are actually more legacies coming through rush than sororities can pledge.

Most sororities shoot pretty straight when talking about legacies, and most national Web sites address legacy status. The consensus seems to be that while legacies are important to sororities and will be afforded consideration during the rush process, it doesn't mean legacies are guaranteed a bid.

Now, before you completely stress out, listen up. We have full details on legacy status coming up, but first, meet two sisters with experiences you can learn from. The ladies have lots in common: they have great jobs, live in cool towns, and oh yes, they were both in sororities in college. In fact, they were in the same sorority, at the same college. And although they had legacy status at one sorority, they ended up pledging a different one. And their roads to sisterhood weren't exactly the same.

Kathryn says rush was a dream. She loved meeting everyone, felt at ease, and knew in her heart she'd find the right place.

But poor Kelly! Kathryn's big sis hit a rough patch on her way to becoming a sorority girl. It was total drama at first—but she ended up making it happen.

Here are their stories, and some words of advice for you. (Names were changed to protect their privacy.)

Kelly's Story

Kelly's picture should be in the dictionary next to the word "success." She majored in interior design at her university's school of architecture, worked for an architecture firm after college, and now has her own business. When builders want to be kind to the environment while putting up their structures, they turn to Kelly and she sets them straight. Smart, hard working, always on the go. Plus, she's just fun to talk to. The kind of girl sororities fight over, right?

Well, recruitment didn't work out for Kelly until the second time around—even though she was a double legacy. On the surface, Kelly's recruitment experience should have been a breeze. She had her recommendations and other paperwork in order, she knew what to wear for each round, and her mother and aunt had been members of one sorority on campus. She was an out-of-state student and didn't know many girls at her school. Before rush even started, she felt confident she would end up at the sorority where she had legacy status.

After the first round, Kelly was cut by a sorority she had really liked. Still, she felt pretty confident that the sorority where she was a legacy was a safe bet. Another surprise—she was cut late in the process. "I thought I had better odds," she said. "It really shook my foundation. It affected my ability to have an open mind through the rest of recruitment."

When it came time to fill out her bid card, Kelly listed only one sorority. It was a big risk, and it didn't work out for her. "I didn't get in the first year," says Kelly. "I just sort of fell through the cracks. It caught me by surprise."

But she didn't let her initial disappointment keep her down, and she approached rush with a different attitude the second time around, as a sophomore. By that time, she knew more girls and felt more connected. "I realized the world wasn't going to fall apart if it wasn't going to happen," says Kelly. "I still really wanted to participate in Greek life, but I realized it wasn't the end of the world. I wasn't as attached to the outcome."

She kept an open mind the second go-round. Rushing again, as a sophomore, was a success. She pledged a sorority—but not the one where she had legacy status. It was the perfect match for her.

Today, Kelly says her sorority experience has helped in her career. She knows how to organize her time, deal with lots of different personalities and "sell" herself to new clients. "It shows you there's value in all people," she says.

Been There, Done That (Twice!): Kelly's Advice

- Don't focus on just one choice, but remain open to all sororities.
- Work on being a good conversationalist. Remember the sorority members have to talk to hundreds of girls and they're likely tired!
- Don't bring up religion, politics, or anything highly controversial.
- Don't judge the sorority or its members until you know more. Don't let other people's opinions influence you.
- Don't talk about money.
- Don't make any enemies. Don't bust on the sororities or their members, even if you're just kidding around.
- Don't wear anything too revealing or sexy.
- Ask the sorority member you're paired up with about herself. Come up with a list of five questions to ask. You just want to keep the conversation going.

Kathryn's Story

Kelly's rough road blazed the trail for her younger sister Kathryn, who rushed her freshman year. "I literally loved every minute of it," Kathryn says

The first round, known at her school as the ice-water tea round, was informal and fun. Kathryn visited all the sororities on campus the first day of recruitment, which was held before classes started. "That night you find out who invited you back the following day," Kathryn explains. "Some cut you, some you get to cut."

Kathryn was a legacy at one sorority and a double legacy at another, and her sister had graduated right before she began her freshman year. By preferential day, Kathryn felt confident. She knew by the third day her favorite choices, she says. "I wasn't that concerned. I had some friends who were just a wreck. I was really calm about it." On bid day, Kathryn got a bid to her top choice. It was all good.

The second quarter of her freshman year, Kathryn moved into the sorority hall (her college doesn't have sorority houses; sisters live together in certain halls in different dorms) and became very active. She became a rush counselor her junior year. Kathryn, who majored in public relations, is now an events planner. She says the leadership and organizational skills she developed during her sorority experience have helped her in her career, while her sorority's requirements helped her during college.

"You have to go to chapter every Wednesday night, you have to keep your grades up," Kathryn says. "It really gives you boundaries that at 18 you don't think you need but you really do need. I'm active in the alumni chapter. It's a great networking tool."

Words of Wisdom from a Former Recruitment Counselor: Kathryn's Advice

● It's really not a life-or-death situation! "Some of the girls had a really tough time," Kathryn says. "They had their heart set on a sorority, and they were dropped. For a lot of those girls, it was devastating." Realize there are other opportunities for you on campus.

When filling out your final preferential card, list all remaining sororities in your order of preference, not just one! You're risking not getting into a sorority at all if you take that route. "If you just put one down and they don't choose you, that's it," Kathryn says. Everyone in her group the year she was a recruitment counselor ended up pledging, including one girl who wrote down only one. Kathryn says she was nearly as nervous as that girl!

Remember sorority members are people, too. "The hardest part is when you're sitting there and thinking, everybody here is perfect, everybody is beautiful, everybody is smart, everybody is dressed to a T," Kathryn says. "Once you get to know them, you're like, okay, these people are real, too. A month after I pledged, I remember looking and thinking, they're so normal. They have faults. They're not as perfect as I thought."

Realize the long-term value of the experience. "You do have to get mentally ready," Kathryn says. "It's kind of how life is. It got me ready for my college experience and for the real world."

Keep an open mind. "There are great girls in all of the sororities," Kathryn says. "Having an open mind is something you really want to try to do."

Kelly and Kathryn were legacies when they went through recruitment, but they did not end up pledging at their mother's sorority. See? Like we said, being a legacy just isn't all that.

If you are a legacy, that's awesome. The sororities initially will take a closer look at you, but it is not the defining ingredient to success. Sorority members want to know about you, not just who you're related to. The point of recruitment is for all potential members and all sororities to find the best mutual matches. Legacy status isn't an "automatic in" —especially if the particular girl just doesn't seem that into the sorority at which she has legacy status.

The most helpful legacy relationship is the most specific. If your mother or sister was a member of the very chapter you are rushing, for example, that's more significant than if they were members of chapters at other schools. Also considered will be whether the relative who provides your legacy status has been an active alumna, remaining involved and volunteering with the sorority.

Sororities typically have rules governing their legacies. For example, if a legacy is cut, the sorority may be required to call the relative who affords the legacy status and explain why the girl was let go. (That's got to be the worst job during recruitment, by the way.) Many sororities have a minimum number of days that they will keep a legacy. If you're a legacy, keep in mind that getting invited back after the first round may reflect sorority policy, rather than your long-term prospects at that sorority.

Take the time to familiarize yourself with sorority policies on legacies by checking with the sorority's national Web site. Generally speaking, a legacy who is invited to the preferential round during rush should be placed on that sorority's top list, and will very likely be offered a bid. On the other hand, legacies can find themselves cut after an early round.

We talked to current and alumnae sorority members regarding legacies. Here's what one young woman had to say about the legacy who rushed her sorority and didn't get a bid: "She was rude to everyone, and acted like she wasn't interested in us at all. She seemed like she just didn't want to be there." Who knows what this girl's deal was? She just didn't have her act together, and she clearly didn't seem into the idea of sorority membership, even though she was a legacy. It was probably best for everyone that she did not end up at this particular sorority.

In most cases, a girl who is a legacy will be as excited to learn about the sorority as the members are to meet her. A girl who pledges the same sorority as her mother, grandmother, or sister can enjoy a particularly special sorority experience.

The same sorority alumna who told us about the horrible, rude legacy had a story with a very happy ending to tell as well. One year during her sorority's rush, members were excited to meet a girl whose mother, sister, and grandmother had all been members of their sorority. The special bond of sorority sisterhood that all generations of women in their family shared was a very heartfelt connection. This family's home was totally decked out in sorority memorabilia. Come Christmastime, their tree was laden with ornaments bearing the sorority's Greek letters —more evidence of their devotion.

"They were one big, happy [XYZ] family!" the member said. When the girl pledged, the entire family (including her new sisters, of course) all celebrated.

Yes, legacies are treated differently. Legacy status gets you a closer first look. Sometimes legacy status can cause potential new members to make up their minds before they even get to campus and start the recruitment process. Remember, this is your time! Keep an open mind, find the fit that is right for you, and don't feel you must choose the sorority a relative was in. If that sorority turns out to be the right place for you, wonderful! But another sorority may be a better fit for you. Remaining open to different possibilities will help ensure you truly find your Greek home.

Legacy status gets you a closer first look, but what you do after that is up to you. It's a piece of the puzzle, but you've got to get the other pieces in place to give sororities the total picture. Don't get upset if you don't have legacy status. Because of the numbers, sororities can't possibly take all the legacies who rush. It's up to each girl to make a connection.

BOTTOM LINE:

Being a legacy can make both you and the sorority take a closer look. Remember to make the choice your own.

CHAPTER TEN

Hook Me Up, Sister!

Hook Me Up, Sister!

Following are six real life stories...

1. The vote is in...a young actress

Dara McCarney is beautiful, talented, and on her way to becoming seriously famous. Her sorority sisters—both at her college and around the country—played a big role in getting her national exposure.

The fall before she graduated, national network reps came to Dara's school, looking for new talent. She auditioned and producers chose her as the school's female winner. Dara was pumped—and her journey was just beginning. Producers flew Dara and the winners from other colleges to New York, where each performed a spot on an early-morning show. Now it was up to the viewers to decide who would win by logging on to cast their votes.

That's when Dara's sorority sisters got busy. Their girl was off the hook, so they got on-line to make sure she won. "It was put on the sorority email," Dara says. "Sisters from all over the country got involved in voting. It definitely had a big influence on how many votes I got."

When Dara was declared the national female winner, her prize was a guest appearance on a top soap opera. She says she knew her sisters at school and nationwide helped put her there, and soon learned that it hadn't been just her sorority sisters voting for her. Sisters spread the word to friends in other sororities, and soon members from a number of sororities (and fraternities) were backing Dara. "It's kind of cool how the whole Greek system was tied in," she says.

Her guest-starring appearance lasted three episodes; Dara played a girl who got set up on a blind date, then hooked up with the valet instead. "It didn't work out," Dara says of the fictional on-screen date. "I wish it had!"

We're sure to be seeing more of Dara in the future. For now, this rising star has some advice. "Stick with it," Dara says. "If it doesn't work out for you, you can always change your mind later."

She went through recruitment and joined as a freshman. Although she went through the process with her two best friends from high school, each joined a different sorority. She made new friends as she maintained friendships from high school and was an active sorority member. "We accomplished a lot in the four years I was there," she says of her sorority.

She does know of some girls who dropped out during recruitment or depledged after joining. Sorority life is not for everyone, and that's okay. "You don't have to join your freshman year," she notes. "You can go back through if it doesn't work out. It's not the end of the world."

Although recruitment can be a draining process, the effort pays off, Dara says. "I promise you, it gets a lot better after rush," says Dara, who starting really enjoying her sorority experience after moving into the house. "It's definitely going to be rewarding in the end. You make friendships that are going to be priceless. I'd do it all over again."

You make friendships that are going to be priceless.

2. From sorority sister to smashing success…a business woman

All right, so you're not into soap operas.

But how about working at a great job after college? Sorority experience can pave the way for professional success.

Jody, an energy company executive on the West Coast, attended a college known for its excellent engineering and technical programs—

and the fact that men far outnumber women on campus. For her, sorority life was a great way to meet gal pals in that sea of testosterone. "My rush experience was extremely positive," she says. "I loved getting dressed up and going to parties to meet new people, and I actually relished the competitiveness of it all. To me it was sport!" (Does that sound like a trait that might come in handy in the business world? It does to us, too!)

Jody says she had an idea of which sorority she might prefer, but kept an open mind during recruitment. She got to know her fellow rushees, and she and her freshman roommate ended up pledging the same sorority. "I made the best friends of my life through my sorority," Jody says, remembering formals and mixers with funny names like the "Mallard Ball" or "Barn Party."

Now that she's in the business world, she realizes that although her sorority was tons of fun, it got her ready for the real world, too. She learned to get along with just about anyone, working together with people from various backgrounds to achieve common goals.

"Joining a sorority also gave me ample opportunity to take on leadership roles, and I held several positions during my tenure," Jody says. "Those positions gave me more confidence to pursue other leadership roles in other organizations in college."

Her sorority did an awesome job making sisters feel recognized at special occasions in their lives, too. "Probably what I learned most from sorority life that helps me in my job today is the ability to recognize that with a large group of people there will always be many opinions, and that you have to respect others while maintaining your sense of self," Jody says.

She has traveled the globe with her job, and says one of the first questions other businesswomen ask is, "Were you in a sorority?" It has made her realize what an important stepping stone sorority life was!

Jody's advice? Pull yourself together as if you were going on a job interview. Be polite. Be yourself. Interview the sorority as much as they are interviewing you, and decide what is important to you in friendships. Look for a sorority that exhibits those qualities.

Find out about each sorority's academic standards. Listen to what people have to say about their reputation on campus and make sure it is aligned with what you are looking for. Are they the party house? The scholastic girls? The Southern belles? The snobs? The rich kids? Make sure that when you do decide on your favorites, that you make it clear you are interested in them. Don't get your feelings hurt when you get cut. Recognize that it is a complicated process.

Most importantly, have fun!

"Joining a sorority also gave me ample opportunity to take on leadership roles"

3. You'll never meet a stranger again...a nationally known speaker

Jean Stafford is president of Executive Coaching for Women (jeanstafford.com), based in the Washington, D.C. area. She speaks to hundreds of women a year and has been interviewed for dozens of national publications. She is a graduate of a university in Texas, where she was an active sorority member. She didn't realize that talking to girls during rush and learning to feel more comfortable around new people, would become so key to her career.

"I really didn't understand the value of meeting so many different people" Stafford says. "I didn't know I was networking. I just thought I was rushing. I never understood how valuable those contacts could be."

Now a prominent businesswoman and nationally known speaker, Stafford says she was uncomfortable at first speaking to people she didn't know during rush. Yet that skill has helped build her professional success. "What I can do is walk into a room of people I don't know, and work the room," she says. "Most of my clients come to me that way."

The advice she gives clients is useful to prospective sorority members, too. "Be capable," Stafford says. "Joining a sorority, you have to be able to meet the requirement of that sorority. Let other people know that you're capable. In my own experience with rush, the women for the various sororities who were rushing me wanted me to tell them what I had to contribute, what value was I going to bring to the sisterhood."

Stafford says a prospective sorority member should make sure a particular chapter meets her goals. "You have to decide for yourself what you want out of the experience of being in sorority," she says. "It's about understanding if you've got a match."

"I didn't know I was networking. I just thought I was rushing. I never understood how valuable those contacts could be."

4. Rush hour ... a fast-track collegian

Recruitment doesn't work out for everyone – and that's okay. Sometimes it's better than okay. Check out this story from a college alumna who decided she couldn't fit the commitment of a sorority into her schedule, but still came away with a positive experience.

"Right before the final round, I was offered an internship I knew would help me land a good job after college. I knew I couldn't do both. I had to choose. Ultimately I decided that the internship was the route for me, but not before I learned a lesson about myself. Rush was going great, and I was getting ready for the third round of parties, when I looked down at my schedule card and realized I'd gotten the time wrong! I now had ten minutes to walk about a mile—in heels! No one had cars on campus, and I had no idea what the bus schedule was. I wasn't giving up, though. I ran outside my dorm and flagged down the first car I saw. It happened to be a pizza delivery truck.

'Please, you've got to drive me to the XYZ house!' I told the poor guy, probably a fellow student. He looked at me like I was nuts and said, 'Sorry, I'm not a taxi service.' He delivered pizza, not rushees! But I was insistent. Somehow I convinced him to shuttle me over there. I had him drop me off down the road, of course, so the group wouldn't see me getting out of a pizza truck. I filed in with the rest of the girls and enjoyed the parties. No one ever knew.

"That night, after the parties had concluded, there was a message on my answering machine: I had been offered this awesome internship. They wanted an answer quickly, and I would need to start right away. I had applied for the internship with no hope of landing it, so I was shocked. I was also sad, because I knew I could not fit both commitments into my schedule. I didn't want to join a sorority unless I knew I could really devote myself to it. To do otherwise seemed disrespectful to all the girls involved, and to the process itself.

"After some soul searching I went to my recruitment counselor. She was supportive although disappointed, and helped me complete the process of discontinuing rush. A few days later, many of my friends were excited to receive bids at great sororities. I didn't have too much time to feel sad at not joining them, because I was so busy. The internship did indeed lead to a great job, and I know I made the right choice.

"Although I didn't end up in a sorority, that rush experience taught me something about myself. It helped me organize my thoughts and prioritize. I considered my choices and planned a clear path for myself. And, let's face it, I never would have dreamed I had the gumption to flag down a pizza delivery truck. Not that I recommend using this as a method of transportation—but the experience left me realizing I can be capable, resourceful, and very persuasive.

"I have fond memories of all the girls I met during rush, of my sweet and helpful recruitment counselor, and of that poor, confused driver who must have thought I was insane!"

"...the experience left me realizing I can be capable, resourceful, and very persuasive."

5. Homecoming... a small-town girl

Here's a story from a woman whose sorority sisters helped her realize how special she is:

"My older sister was one of those Miss Everything types. You know—Homecoming Court and Miss This and That. I can close my eyes right now and see myself standing on a curb while she passes by in a convertible waving. She has always been very beautiful, and I idolized her from the beginning. She left home to attend a small Southern university while I continued my rather mediocre high school existence. Naturally she excelled in college and did the sorority thing and the beauty queen thing and loved every minute of it. When my time came around, to no one's surprise I attended the same small university and shockingly enough, pledged the same sorority.

"Everything went along in a rather normal fashion until my junior year in college. To my shock and surprise I was nominated by my sorority sisters to be my sorority's homecoming representative. Well, I tried to talk my way out of this but unbelievably ended up agreeing. To this day, I have no understanding of what got into me. Now the hard work began. Back then, you started with a luncheon where you were photographed and interviewed by The Newspaper. Not the little local newspaper (well, that one, too), but the Big Newspaper. Then, God forbid, you were in a pageant and voted on and then presented on the field of the homecoming football game where the queen was announced.

"Well, I made it through the luncheon, piece of cake. But the pageant presented some challenges. First of all, I did not have a formal dress, but never fear – the last homecoming queen had been in my sorority. So I was whisked off to her house to borrow a dress. Well, let me tell you this girl was absolutely beautiful and had been in everything and usually won whatever she was in. I had done something right in my life because we were the same size.

"I entered her bedroom and she opened the closet. It was full of gorgeous long designer dresses. I tried on all the dresses and I had a committee of friends decide which one I should wear. They chose a beautiful black dress from a famous designer. I made it back to the dorm, questioning my sanity along the way. Somehow they had convinced me I could put this dress on, walk across a stage, and live to tell about it.

"The pageant was that night, and I could not imagine how I was going to manage to get through the experience. As I walked onto the sorority hall and headed toward my room, I was completely shocked. My door was covered in good luck signs and crepe paper and glitter. My room was filled with flowers and covered from floor to ceiling with decorations. I stood there with barely enough room to turn around. I have never to this day felt as loved and supported by so many people at one time. Well, it got me in the dress and to the auditorium. I'm sure I was in a state of shock. As I stood on stage looking at nothing but bright lights, I wondered what was going to get me to the end of the stage and back. I heard my name and as I started forward I was overwhelmed by thunderous applause and cheering. I made it to the end of the stage and I saw all of my sorority sisters and all of the brothers of the fraternity where I was a little sister standing and cheering for me. Well, I lived through it. I didn't win, and I can't remember who did, but the experience still gives me chills because there has never been another time that I felt so much love and support from so many people."

> "... I felt so much love and support from so many people."

6. The sweetheart song...a business executive

One woman said she realized the true value of sorority membership long after she left campus. Here is her story:

"As much as I enjoyed my years as a sorority sister, it was a moment years later that really captured how special my Greek experience was.

"I was a guest speaker at a business conference at the Peabody Hotel in Memphis. While waiting for a colleague in the restaurant I noticed a group of young men talking and laughing. It was obviously some type of reunion because they were proudly wearing their Greek letters. Some of the best times of my college days were as a little sister for the same fraternity.

"The sight of this group made me smile as I remembered the exciting parties and special ceremonies I shared with my sorority and fraternity friends during college. As a freshman at my state college, everything seemed so overwhelming. I had been active in student government and club leadership in high school but those groups at the college level seemed enormous and far away. Before college, I didn't know anything about sororities or fraternities or what it could mean to me. It turned out, going Greek gave me an outlet for social activities and helped me connect with my college. I had tons of fun!

"Thinking about all those happy times, I asked my waiter to anonymously charge the young businessmen's beverages to my bill. My colleague arrived, we began our dinner meeting, and reviewed our conference plans for the next day. The group of young men and my college days were forgotten. After my colleague and I finished our dinner and were preparing to leave, the group of young men circled my table with smiles on their faces. They began to serenade me with the fraternity "Sweetheart Song," right there in the restaurant of that elegant hotel. Glancing up at the other restaurant patrons, all I could see were warm, touching smiles as all eyes focused on our table.

"At that moment, years after college was over, I got it. With this chance encounter I internalized just how special Greek membership is. You are connected. A member of a family, steeped in tradition and timeless in its ability to make you feel a part of something that is larger than yourself. That lesson will be with me always. Maybe it is a lesson you will know as well."

"With this chance encounter I internalized just how special Greek membership is."

BOTTOM LINE:

The world's all about connections —
sororities are a great place to start.

What's your special story? Share it at
www.sororityguide.com!

CHAPTER ELEVEN

Dear Mom and Dad:

Advice for Parents and a Brief History of Sororities

Dear Mom and Dad: Advice for Parents and a Brief History of Sororities

You may be reeling from sticker shock before your daughter sets foot on campus. You've paid for SAT prep classes, college visits, and application fees. Tuition bills are headed your way. (If they're coming from out of state, you're really feeling the bite.)

Now that your daughter knows where she's going to college, she's considering Greek life. You're naturally wondering, what's in it for my daughter? Should I really pay money for her to have friends?

One important thing you can do is help your daughter look at everything she's going to be involved in and help her decide if she has the time to dedicate to sorority membership. If your daughter has been the type of high school student who is involved in just about every club and organization and she's looking for ways to connect with smaller groups at college, sorority life may be just the thing. If, on other hand, she is on a traveling sports or cheerleading team, plays in the marching band, or is part of another organization that requires a huge time commitment, help her realistically assess whether she has room in her life for sorority membership. Help her realize that she's not going to simply join, then show up for parties! Sorority membership, especially as a pledge, will require her to spend a certain amount of time at meetings, in study hall, even at social events. If your daughter's sorority supports a house, she will likely be required to eat meals there or actually live there.

Keep in mind, the amount of Greek information on college Web sites varies. Some might be very comprehensive, others are light on details.

You've got lots of questions. We've got lots of answers.

What are the benefits of Greek life?

When she says Greek, are you thinking about movies like "Animal House" or "Old School"? Are you wondering if you're paying just for partying?

While there are tons of fun activities associated with Greek life, sororities also encourage many of the values that you as a parent have worked hard for many years to instill in your daughters. Sorority members generally have stricter rules to abide by than non-Greek college students.

- Sorority life is like a social and academic safety net. The chapter will have standards, and members are accountable to their sisters for their grades and behavior.

- Local chapters at your daughter's school have many positions, such as big sisters, chaplain, and standards committees, to support and enforce the ideals upon which the sorority is founded.

- Local chapters are overseen by the Panhellenic office at the college and by the national headquarters of the sorority. National policies banning hazing or underage drinking support local chapters and provide standards.

- Greek members have more opportunities to get involved in intramural sports including softball, tennis, and lacrosse. If your daughter isn't going out for the varsity team but still wants to remain involved in her favorite sport, this is a great way for her to stay in the game.

- Sororities are prohibited from serving alcohol during recruitment, and many support dry social functions throughout the year.

  Sorority life is a time-tested method of encouraging common goals, values, and traditions through friendship and sisterhood.

Will her grades be affected?

Yes—for the better! Sororities have minimum grade requirements to join, and require that their members maintain a certain GPA. Studies show that members of Greek organizations have higher GPAs and a higher percentage of students who complete college. Trust us—you can find this information on the colleges' Web sites. Greek organizations are proud of their strict academic standards and success. Details will be highlighted on the Greek pages of her school's Web site.

Other thoughts on grades:

- Sororities have mandatory study hour programs and often have tutoring available for their members.

- The chapters often keep copies of old tests and exams on file for use as study aids by their members.

- If a member does not keep up her grades she may face academic probation and not be allowed to attend social functions until her grades improve. That's a powerful incentive to hit the books!

- Sororities require pledges to maintain a minimum GPA established by their national headquarters in order to be formally initiated.

What's this going to cost?

It's hard to say exactly what you'll pay for sorority membership. Fees vary widely from school to school and from sorority to sorority. Financial details specific to your daughter's college should be available on the school's Web site. Some sororities include a list of itemized expenses on their sites. Others provide only general cost estimates. Either way, your daughter will find out what her sorority's fee schedule is during pledge period.

The most significant factor in cost is whether the sorority has to support a house. You can expect to pay at least double, maybe four times as much, for a sorority that has its own house. Remember, though, living in the house and participating in its meal plan would replace the cost of housing and meal plans on campus.

Before selling all your daughter's things on eBay to raise money, consider that Greek living can actually be less expensive than other arrangements. One West Coast college we looked at calculated that the average per semester for a sorority member living in the house was about $2,250, including room, board, and all dues and fees. A comparable residence hall and campus meal plan would cost about $3,250 per semester, the school figured.

In comparison, at a major Southern university where sororities don't have houses to pay for, the cost of membership is much lower: $750 to $1,200 per year.

Fill out the chart as you consider different sororities, and compare costs for yourself ...

COLLEGE / UNIVERSITY:			
Sororities with Houses	Dues/Fees	Living Expenses	TOTAL
XY	1150	1100	2250

COLLEGE / UNIVERSITY:			
Sororities with Chapter Rooms	Dues/Fees	Living Expenses	TOTAL
ZYX	1100	N/A	1100

Here's a breakdown of the various costs associated with sorority membership:

Recruitment fee. This covers the cost of recruitment materials. It must be included with your daughter's registration materials and can usually be paid via credit card on-line. Some campuses require electronic payments. Schools that accept checks will include payment information, including an address to mail a payment or a link for on-line payments on the college Web site. This varies from school to school. The fee can be as low as $10 to as high as $100. The average recruitment fee range is $30 to $50.

Pledge/new member fee. This is a one-time cost paid soon after recruitment ends. It'll likely be around $100, although the range varies, not only from school to school but also from house to house. At some sororities the pledge fee is higher, around $200 or more, but semester dues are subsequently lower.

Initiation fee. This is also a one-time cost, paid at the time when pledges are initiated. At some sororities, this fee includes the pin. At others the pin fee is separate. This fee really varies from school to school. At colleges where sororities have houses, the initiation fee can be $200, $300, or higher. At colleges where sororities are located in residence halls instead of separate houses, this fee is typically less than $100.

House/parlor fee. This also varies among colleges and sororities. One major Southern university, for example, has fourteen sororities on campus. Their house fees range from $0 to more than $700—quite a difference. The house fee reflects the sorority's physical property. If it's a brand-new house, unusually large, or undergoing extensive renovations, you can expect a bigger house fee. Some houses charge a separate fee for security guards.

Meal plans. If the sororities support a house, they generally require members to participate in their meal plans, and these are often close to what the campus meal plans cost. Depending on the type of plan selected this can range from under $400 to more than $1,000 per semester.

Housing. Depending on your daughter's sorority, she may be required to live in the house for a certain number of semesters. This cost also will often correlate to housing costs on campus. In some cases, living in the house can be very comparable—even less expensive—than other housing options. It can certainly be less expensive than an off-campus apartment. A typical range is $700 to $1,000 per semester, but this is different at every school and every sorority.

Dues. These cover chapter operating expenses, payments to the sorority's national office, and some social functions. Around $500 is a ballpark average. At some schools you'll pay between $200 and $300. At others, dues can be to $700 or higher. In some cases, dues cover all socials, as well as items like T-shirts and photos. At other schools, those items are paid for separately.

Social expenses

T-shirts. What would sorority life be without a T-shirt for every day of the week? Okay, that's a bit of an exaggeration. But you'll be amazed at the number of shirts your daughter soon accumulates. T-shirts commemorating functions like Derby Days, Greek Week, spring formals, and more usually cost $10 to $15 for short-sleeve, about $20 for long-sleeve. If not included in dues, these can add up. Talk to your daughter about selecting a few events to remember with a T-shirt, instead of purchasing one for each and every event.

Photos. Another sorority must! When sororities hold mixers, theme parties, semi-formals, and formals, the guest of honor at each event is the photographer. Later, composites are displayed and members can choose photos they'd like to purchase. The cost is usually only a couple dollars per picture, but this, too, can add up quickly. Here's a thought: Have your daughter foot the bill for photos and T-shirts. That may help her decide which ones she really wants.

If you're concerned about cost, suggest your daughter work over the summer to help pay for her sorority. It's a good lesson in money management for her to learn now.

How much time is this going to take?

As we've stated, sorority membership is a big time commitment. Your daughter will need to be prepared to attend mandatory chapter meetings and pledge meetings, to eat most of her meals at the house if her sorority has one, and to log a certain number of hours studying. That's right! Sororities often require their members to spend a specified number of hours each week in study hall.

She'll be expected to participate in sorority social functions and charity events. Some of these are mandatory. Perhaps most important, your daughter is going to be expected to conduct herself appropriately at all times. Sororities want their members to enjoy college and express their individuality, but they also expect members to project a positive image. Membership in a sorority can give you peace of mind that your daughter will have a good group of girls encouraging her to make good and responsible choices throughout her college years.

By the numbers

According to the National Panhellenic Conference, in 2005 there were:

* 3,612,176 members

* 80,336 new members

* 2,908 college chapters

* 4,678 alumnae chapters

Sorority members are generous with their time and resources both while in college and after graduation. The NPC reports that:

✳ Over a two-year period, 552 college chapters completed more than 329,000 service hours and donated more than $5 million to community projects, and ...

✳ During the 2003-04 school year, 213 alumnae chapters gave more than $445,000 in scholarships and grants to more than 500 recipients.

What about Safety?

The media occasionally report a sensational account of young women who have bad experiences with sororities. From shocking headlines to "tell-all" exposes, it's easy to become concerned about just exactly what sorority life might involve.

Talk to your daughter about stories in the media. Make sure she knows she is too valuable and too smart to agree to any behavior that's dangerous or illegal. Sorority membership should be a fun, positive experience. If something doesn't feel right, she should walk away. If she feels pressured to engage in a dangerous activity, she needs to report it to authorities on her campus. The bottom line: She is more important, ultimately, than any sorority.

The age at which young women consider sorority membership is a volatile time. Just about any young woman is going to be influenced by peer pressure, the desire to be accepted by others, and a fervent wish to fit in and be popular. Issues students may face during this transitional time include depression, eating disorders, and the temptation to abuse alcohol or drugs. Sexual abuse can also be an issue on college campuses. It should comfort you to know that these are all issues sororities are proactive in addressing through training for their members, support committees, and communication with parents.

While you do need to let go as your daughter leaves for college, it's a good idea to check in during recruitment and afterward. Keep an eye out for drastic weight loss, lethargy, severe mood swings—anything that tells you things just aren't right. Campuses are equipped to help students combat depression, eating disorders, substance abuse, and other troubles. Keep in frequent contact. If things seem serious, step in and make sure she gets the help she needs, whether it's a college counselor, a visit to student health, an appointment with your family doctor, or a visit with your family's pastor, priest, or rabbi.

One final thought: Underage drinking and sexual abuse are illegal, and perpetrators can go to jail. Make sure your daughter understands those points very clearly. No sorority is worth your daughter compromising her values, and certainly not worth condoning or participating in any illegal activity. Make sure your daughter knows that anyone who pressures her to drink if she is underage or attempts any sort of unwanted sexual advance is breaking the law and could face legal action. And make sure she knows where to report such incidents.

The sororities on your daughter's college campuses are as varied and diverse as the young women who will be entering the recruitment process. Their different traditions, symbols, and philanthropic goals reflect a wide range of interests. But if sororities have one thing in common, it's bans on hazing.

The commitment to ensure potential new members a recruitment and pledge experience free from pressure to engage in dangerous, humiliating, or embarrassing activities—hazing—starts at the top. The National Panhellenic Conference Web site (www.npcwomen.org) links to a Web site promoting National Hazing Prevention Week (www.nhpw.com). Additionally, all member organizations of the National Panhellenic Conference have adopted policies that support or encourage alcohol-free social events.

The National Pan-Hellenic Council, which includes historically African American fraternities and sororities, has a strongly worded resolution condemning hazing on its Web site, www.nphchq.org. The resolution defines hazing as "any action taken or situation created that involves or results in abusive physical contact or mutual harassment of a prospective Fraternity or Sorority member" and specifies penalties, including legal action or expulsion for members found guilty of hazing.

The National Pan-Hellenic Council sororities in particular do not play around when it comes to hazing. Break the rules and the ladies will not only toss you out—they'll subject you to national scorn. Included on their Web sites are members, listed by name, who have been suspended or banned because they ran afoul of sorority rules.

Hazing and related issues also are often addressed on individual sororities' Web sites. On many sites, there's a special link for parents to educate moms and dads about no-tolerance policies on hazing, as well as other topics. Every site includes contact information if you want more specific details.

Yes, there have been reported cases of hazing, but these isolated events routinely draw swift and serious sanctions from the schools at which they occur, and legal action sometimes follows. Internet access makes it easier to research hazing policies—and easier to stumble across sensational accounts of just about any occurrence.

And by the way, not everything you read in the newspaper turns out to be accurate. One very high-profile article alleged all sorts of terrible hazing going on at a major West Coast university. Not long after the article ran, the reporter was fired and the respected, Pulitzer-prize winning newspaper had to run a lengthy correction. If you run across sensational headlines, take the time to keep up with continuing coverage of the story, if you're concerned. It may turn out to be overblown, exaggerated, or not true at all.

Of course, anti-hazing policies and conferences wouldn't exist if there wasn't a need to address the problem. Arm yourself with facts, not gossip, and talk to your daughter before she leaves for school. She should know her safety and well-being is more important than membership in any group, and together you should identify the person or department responsible for addressing hazing allegations at your daughter's school. Send her to college with that phone number or email address, and make sure she feels confident enough that, should the unthinkable occur, she will not hesitate to make a report. With sororities' proactive stance on banning hazing, it's likely she won't need to.

Where do I turn for help?

If you feel your daughter may need more help than you as a loving parent can provide, here is a list of resources:

The National Association of Anorexia Nervosa and Associated Disorders offers hotline counseling, a national network of free support groups, referrals to health care professionals, and education and prevention programs: www.anad.org or 847-831-3438.

The Eating Disorder Referral and Information Center offers comprehensive information, including referral information: www.edreferral.com.

The National Institutes of Health Web site offers excellent information, including the latest research, on a wide range of medical issues, including depression: www.nih. gov.

The National Institute on Alcohol Abuse and Alcoholism's Web site offers a wealth of information, including studies on drinking by college fraternity and sorority members: www.niaaa.nih.gov.

How do I support her through recruitment?

- Be available for phone calls.

- Don't push a particular sorority. Your sorority experience was great for you, but this is her time.

- Remember your daughter has many gifts and talents. She'll have plenty of places to put them to work.

▨ One well-publicized incident should not deter your daughter from pursuing sorority life. Coverage of one traffic accident isn't going to keep you from driving her to school, is it? Still, this is an emotionally volatile age, and sorority recruitment compresses highs, lows, anxiety, excitement, elation, and possible disappointment into a short and stressful time period.

▨ Sorority members are no different than any group of young college women, in that they occasionally deal with emotional or physical stresses. Be there for your daughter during this time and afterward. Let her know that no matter what, you love and support her.

How can I help her deal with disappointment?

An article in a major newspaper detailed the difficulty some parents have in "letting go" when their children leave for college. There was the mom who emailed her daughter daily to remind her about upcoming tests and papers, and the mom who actually drove to her child's campus weekly just to check in. Then there was the mom who called the office of the dean of students freaking out because her daughter did not get a bid at the sorority she sought. It was worse than being diagnosed with a life-threatening illness, this drama queen cried.

Really, now.

As important—even crucial—as your daughter's recruitment and sorority experience seems, it's important to keep a level head and maintain perspective. Sorority life is just one part of your daughter's overall college experience, and a disappointing recruitment process is not the end of her world or yours.

What to do if recruitment doesn't go her way

- Remind her why she went to college: she's there for an education.
- Encourage her to get involved in other activities.
- Help her realize her she's more important that any sorority.
- Talk about this as a character-building experience.
- Let her know how much you love and support her.
- Sometimes, just listening is the most important thing you can do.

BOTTOM LINE:

"Parents just have to be supportive and also realize it's not the end of the world. It's a small thing in the scheme of things."

– Dr. Jean Twenge, San Diego State University

Where do I go for more information?

- Pay close attention to all materials that come from your daughter's college. Information about recruitment will start arriving as early as the fall before school begins.

- Attend the parents' orientation, and make sure to attend programs dealing with recruitment. If none are listed, ask the event organizers whom you should call on campus.

- Search the college Web site. If it's not immediately apparent where information on sororities is located, search under "student life" or "student organizations." Or type the word "Greek" or "sorority" into the site's search engine. If that doesn't work, call for help.

- Read the National Panhellenic Conference Web site, www.npcwomen.org. That site will direct you to individual sororities' sites, where you can learn more about each one.

- Seek out Greek alumnae sites for groups in your area. Those members can offer guidance and may even be willing to write recommendations for your daughter.

- Ask around! You never know which of your friends, co-workers, or fellow church or PTA members might be great Greek resources.

Five things to look forward to as a sorority parent...

1. **Parents' Weekend**, when you'll have a chance to visit the sorority house or chapter room, meet some of your daughter's new friends, and get an idea of what her college experience is like.

2. **Good report cards.** Sororities typically require their members to maintain certain grade point averages or face social probation or other sanctions. That incentive may be even more powerful than your encouragement to work on keeping up that GPA.

3. Peace of mind that comes from knowing your daughter is associating with girls who place importance on good values, proper behavior, philanthropic endeavors, and lifelong sisterhood.

4. Mother's pins, treasured adornments that signify the special relationship between moms and daughters in the context of sisterhood.

5. A ton of T-shirts to wash and photos to admire every time she comes home!

What's the History of Sororities?

The founders of the first societies for women were bright, resourceful and driven by their devotion to one another and to ideals of friendship and virtue. Wesleyan College in Macon, Georgia, was chartered in December of 1836, with classes starting in January of 1839. It was the first college in the nation to grant degrees to women. It also claims the first two sororities. Tena Roberts, a retired archivist at Wesleyan, shared her knowledge in this area.

Alpha Delta Pi started as the Adelphean Society. It was founded at Wesleyan in 1851 by Eugenia Tucker. The charter members were her close friends. Phi Mu, which started as the Philomathean Society, was founded there in 1852. The founders were Mary Ann DuPont, Mary Elizabeth Myrick, and Martha Bibb Hardaway. "They were encouraged and helped by members of the faculty," Roberts said.

The Adelphean Society became a national organization in 1898 and changed its name to Alpha Delta Phi in 1905 and to Alpha Delta Pi in 1913. The Philomathean Society became a national organization with Greek letters in 1905.

Today, early memorabilia, including badges, pins, and portraits of the founders are on display at the Cannonball House in Macon. But you won't find ADPi or Phi Mu houses anywhere on the Wesleyan campus. In 1913, the college trustees voted to ban sororities, declaring them to be too disruptive, Roberts said. A few years after that vote, the last ADPi and Phi Mu members graduated, effectively closing the chapters at the school where the organizations were founded.

Monmouth College in Illinois is where two more of the country's societies for women, Pi Beta Phi and Kappa Kappa Gamma, were founded. Jeff Rankin, communications director at Monmouth College and the school's "unofficial historian," has thoroughly researched the formation of the first sorority.

The year was 1867. The country had just been through the Civil War, a time when young men were more likely to be serving in the military than attending college. Monmouth College, unique in that it has always been co-ed, stayed open during the war due to the perseverance of the female students. "The women kept the college going," Rankin said. "I wouldn't be surprised if that didn't give them a sense of independence."

During the war, the Monmouth men learned of Greek organizations from their association with young men from various eastern states. Upon their return, they began forming fraternities as was the custom in eastern colleges. It wasn't long before the Monmouth women decided they wanted to go Greek. "The women were starting to get a little jealous," Rankin said.

At that time the only social activity involved the literary society (debates with neighboring schools stirred rivalries like football or basketball games do today). And all students attended regular Chapel services. David Wallace, the school's first president, was also a Presbyterian minister. "He didn't like the idea of young ladies being escorted to chapel by gentlemen," Rankin said. "He thought that wasn't proper at all."

In a lecture, President Wallace said it would be far better for the young women to serve as their own "independent chaperones" rather than arrive at Chapel on the arms of young men. He had no idea how powerful that statement would turn out to be.

"One of these young ladies, Libbie Brook, heard this, and with another one of her friends, said, 'Let's take him up on that,'" Rankin said.

Libbie Brook lived with some friends a few blocks from campus in an upstairs bedroom in the house of Jacob Holt, who was mayor of Monmouth. In that bedroom, the girls planned a secret society for women. On April 28, 1867, their organization, I.C. Sorosis, was officially founded. (Rankin suspects the I.C. stood for "independent chaperone," perhaps meant to tweak President Wallace.)

The girls ordered special pins from a jeweler in Boston and arrived at Chapel together, wearing the pins in their hair. "It was quite a spectacle," Rankin said. They later renamed the organization Pi Beta Phi, choosing Greek letters as was the custom of fraternities.

Three years after Pi Beta Phi was founded, a second organization for women, Kappa Kappa Gamma, was started at Monmouth. The founder was Minnie Stewart. Her father was a judge who helped craft the charter documents.

President Wallace's own daughter, Elizabeth, became a member of Kappa Kappa Gamma a few years later. As a former fraternity man from his college days at Miami of Ohio, he apparently didn't mind. Neither, evidently, did the young men on campus. "They wrote it up in the student newspaper," Rankin said. "Young men thought it was a pretty neat thing."

Pi Phi's and Kappa's national organizations own and maintain the Holt House and the Minnie Stewart House, respectively. Each year members of both groups attend the "Monmouth Duo" banquet, signifying their shared histories at Monmouth College. Rankin also notes that both organizations officially refer to themselves as "women's fraternities," as do many other groups commonly referred to as sororities.

Although Monmouth is proud of its place in sorority history, for many years the organizations existed in secret. Monmouth banned all fraternities and sororities in 1878. "As a Presbyterian school, it was decided it was of the devil," Rankin said. That sentiment persisted for nearly 40 years, until 1922, when Greek organizations were once again openly permitted at Monmouth. Thanks to the efforts of alumnae members, the sororities founded at the college kept going, and their history and documents were preserved.

The rush parties your daughter will attend, the fun and festive atmosphere of bid day, and the emphasis on service, academic excellence, and lifelong friendship that modern sororities exhibit today are all legacies of young women who were inspired to form the group that led to the myriad sororities on campuses today. Think of them as your daughter begins her own journey through Greek life!

CHAPTER TWELVE

A Greek's Life

A Greek's Life

We talked to current sorority sisters and alumnae from different schools about their experiences during rush and throughout college and beyond. They shared their memories and their advice.

Top ten reasons to join a sorority:

1. **People.** It's a great way to meet people, make your campus seem smaller, and have an "instant social life." This can be especially important if you're going out of state to school, or to a college where you won't know many people from high school. One alumna noted her college had way more guys than girls on campus, so sorority life was a good way to make female friends.

2. **Safety.** Sorority membership ensures that when you do go out you're surrounded by friends with values similar to yours, and you won't have to risk walking around campus alone at night.

3. **Grades.** It provides a powerful incentive to keep up your grades. Sororities require their members to maintain a certain GPA or face social probation. Think about it: You don't want to be paying chapter dues when you can't even attend mixers because you're on academic probation, do you?

4. **Leadership.** You'll have many opportunities for leadership that will provide great material to showcase on your resume in a few years. Sorority life is a good way to learn how to work with other people on common projects. You'll find interests that may help you discover the career that's right for you. You will also develop skills that will help you in that career.

5. **Fashion.** It forces you to build a real wardrobe of outfits suitable for casual, professional, or formal events. (And, of course, you'll graduate with hundreds of sorority T-shirts!)

6. **Self-confidence.** You'll build self-confidence and poise, essential tools when you begin your career.

7. **Talents.** You may discover hidden talents, such as singing, dancing, or T-shirt design! (see #5.)

8. **Memories.** You'll rack up a ton of hilarious college memories during theme parties and mixers.

9. **Self-discovery.** Articulating why you want to be in a sorority and what you feel you bring to the group will help you find out who you really are.

10. **Friends.** Most importantly, you'll make friends for life, girls who will later stand up with you on your wedding day, get together for fun weekends at the beach or mountains, and relive your college experiences during alumnae reunions.

The inside scoop from alumnae members

Q: What traits did you strengthen as a result of sorority membership?

A: Joining a sorority gave me ample opportunity to take on leadership roles. Those positions gave me more confidence to pursue leadership roles in other organizations in college.

Q: How did your sorority sisters make you feel special?

A: Sororities focus on and recognize academic and leadership achievements. It was very rewarding to get honored by my sorority in our chapter meetings every time I made the Dean's list, got a 4.0, or was elected to a collegiate honors society.

Q: What are some other ways sororities support their members?

A: We had candle lighting ceremonies for special occasions, such as when girls announced engagements. We all celebrated when a girl won a college pageant, got elected to the homecoming court, or were accepted into law school or graduate school.

Q: What is the most significant lesson sorority membership has taught you?

A: Probably what I learned most from sorority life that helps me in my job today is the ability to recognize that with a large group of people there will always be many opinions, and that you have to respect others while maintaining your sense of self.

Q: Is legacy status important?

A: That's changing. It used to be really key but there are so many girls now who are legacies. It's definitely not a guarantee. It doesn't give you that big of a boost unless you're a legacy of someone who was in that particular chapter. I wouldn't worry too much if you're not a legacy.

Q: As a sorority member participating in rush, are there things you're looking for in a potential new member?

A: Basically girls who are fun, who are interesting and who want to be there. Girls who will bring a particular strength to the chapter.

Q: Are there things you're wary of as a sorority member considering rushees?

A: A girl who gives the impression that there's going to be a conflict, like her boyfriend lives in another town and they plan to spend every weekend visiting. Or someone who says she hates dressing up—that shows she's not going to get into formals and other social functions.

Q: How does sorority experience compare with everything else you did during college?

A: My sorority was one of many activities I was into during college. I worked part time, completed a broadcasting internship, made dean's list, and took acting classes. I had a ton of fun, but my Greek experience was the best part.

Q: Is money important?

A: Sorority experience is priceless, but membership isn't free. The cost of living in the house and participating in the meal plan takes the place of living in the dorm and participating in the campus meal plan.

Q: How do you handle the disappointment of being cut during the process?

A: Keep in mind it may not be personal. It's all about the numbers in many cases. Don't let the disappointment of not getting invited back to one particular house keep you from really getting to know the girls at another. Focus on the positive each day.

Q: What are some of the long-term benefits of sorority membership?

A: You'll know how to write your resume, and how to present yourself to new people. You'll have experience in working with lots of different people, and you may have held leadership positions. Sorority experience can develop talents and skills you can put to use in the business world. It gives you an opportunity to connect with colleagues. Although the percentage of people who participate in Greek life is small, those are often the most successful people after college.

Q: What words of wisdom do you have for potential new members?

A: My advice to a young woman preparing for rush is pull yourself together as if you were going on a job interview. Be polite. Be yourself. Interview the sorority as much as they interview you. Decide what is important to you in friendships, and look for a house that exhibits those qualities. Make sure that when you do decide on your favorite houses that you make it clear you are interested in them.

Q: What's the most important thing to keep in mind during recruitment?

A: Don't get your feelings hurt when you get cut from a sorority. Recognize that it is a complicated process. Most importantly, have fun!

CHAPTER THIRTEEN

It's Greek to Me

It's Greek to Me

Fun facts and the Greek alphabet
from Alpha to Omega

Hey did you know...

Sororities collectively donate hundreds of thousands of dollars to worthy charities each year, a practice that benefits great causes and develops leadership skills in the women who participate in the philanthropic campaigns.

Sororities have minimum GPAs for joining and remaining a member in good standing.

The Alpha Chi Omega symbol, the lyre, can be found on the set of the TV sitcom Friends.

Alpha Gamma Delta was the first sorority to adopt a signature philanthropy.

Sororities ban alcohol from formal recruitment events and support dry social events throughout the year.

The Coca-Cola colors are red and white because the wife of one of the founders was an Alpha Omega Pi.

At the University of Arkansas in the 1960s, members of the band the Kingsmen, who were Kappa Sigmas, wrote the song "Louie Louie" for the members of Chi Omega.

Astronaut Neil Armstrong took his Phi Delta Theta fraternity pin to the moon.

The word sorority was coined in 1882 for Gamma Phi Beta sorority.

The fleur-di-lis symbol on the Campbell's Soup Can was placed there by a company executive whose wife was a Kappa Kappa Gamma.

Sorority members are more likely to be involved in campus clubs and activities and are active alumni, giving back to their alma maters after graduation.

The film Steel Magnolias is based on the life of a Phi Mu named Shelby. The wedding colors are pink and white in the movie.

Sorority women tend to have above-average GPAs. A college's Web site may include the average campus GPA versus the average Greek GPA.

An arrow can be found on the Wrigley's Spearmint Gum package in honor of the company founder's wife, who was a Pi Beta Phi.

The screenwriter for The Little Mermaid was a Zeta Tau Alpha, and the sorority's symbol, the five-point crown, appears throughout the animated film.

Famous fraternity members include Brad Pitt, who was a sorority sweetheart. (See the Star Power section for more famous Greeks!)

Colleges all across the county have "zero-tolerance" policies in place that ban hazing, and many have hotlines set up to report hazing incidents.

About three percent of United States college students are Greek, but that three percent is a powerful and successful bunch!

Forty-eight percent of all United States presidents have been fraternity men.

More than half of U.S. Senators and more than a third of U.S. Congress members were fraternity or sorority members during their college years.

The first American female astronaut to travel into outer space, Dr. Sally Ride, was a sorority member.

Sororities often have tutoring programs, and they keep materials such as old tests and exams on files as study aids for their members.

The Greek Alphabet

Sororities' use of Greek letters followed fraternities' use of Greek letters. The first Greek organizations were founded at a time when Greek was commonly taught in schools and colleges.

A	Alpha	al-fah		N	Nu	new
B	Beta	bay-tah		Ξ	Xi	zi
Γ	Gamma	gam-ah		O	Omicron	om-i-cron
Δ	Delta	del-tah		Π	Pi	pie
E	Epsilon	ep-si-lon		P	Rho	row
Z	Zeta	zay-tah		Σ	Sigma	sig-mah
H	Eta	ay-tah		T	Tau	taw
Θ	Theta	thay-tah		Υ	Upsilon	oop-si-lon
I	Iota	i-o-tah		Φ	Phi	fie
K	Kappa	kap-pah		X	Chi	kie
Λ	Lambda	lam-dah		Ψ	Psi	sigh
M	Mu	mew		Ω	Omega	o-may-gah

CHAPTER FOURTEEN

A Greek Home for Everyone

A Greek Home for Everyone

There are more choices than ever today
for the girl who's going Greek.

The member organizations of the National Panhellenic Conference

Founded in 1902, the National Panhellenic Conference is an organization that oversees the Greek-letter societies for women on college campuses throughout the country. (Many are officially known as fraternities for women.) The NPC sets national standards for collegiate chapters of sororities represented by the organization. Here is a list of the organizations, a little about them, and Web addresses where you can seek more information, such as their main philanthropic goals, history, and information on founders. The Web site will give you a look at the sorority from a national perspective.

ΑΧΩ
Alpha Chi Omega
Founded: 1885
Colors: Scarlet and olive green
Flower: Red carnation
Web site: www.alphachiomega.org

ΑΔΠ
Alpha Delta Pi
Founded: 1851
Colors: Azure blue and white
Flower: Woodland violet
Web site: www.alphadeltapi.org

ΑΕΦ
Alpha Epsilon Phi
Founded: 1909
Colors: Green and white
Flower: Lily of the valley
Web site: www.aephi.org

ΑΓΔ

Alpha Gamma Delta
Founded: 1904
Colors: Red, buff and green
Flower: A red and buff rose with green asparagus
   plumosa fern
Web site: www.alphagammadelta.org

ΑΟΠ

Alpha Omicron Pi
Founded: 1897
Color: Cardinal
Flower: Jacqueminot (deep red) rose
Web site: www.alphaomicronpi.org

ΑΦ

Alpha Phi
Founded: 1872
Colors: Silver and bordeaux
Flower: Lily-of-the-valley and the blue and gold
   forget-me-not
Web site: www.alphaphi.org

ΑΣΑ

Alpha Sigma Alpha
Founded: 1901
Colors: Crimson and pearl white
Flower: Aster (fall) and narcissus (spring)
Web site: www.alphasigmaalpha.org

ΑΣΤ

Alpha Sigma Tau
Founded: 1899
Colors: Emerald green and gold
Flower: Yellow rose
Web site: www.alphasigmatau.org

ΑΞΔ

Alpha Xi Delta
Founded: 1893
Colors: Double blue (light and dark) and gold
Flower: Pink rose
Web site: www.alphaxidelta.org

ΧΩ

Chi Omega
Founded: 1895
Colors: Cardinal and straw
Flower: White carnation
Web site: www.chiomega.com

ΔΔΔ

Delta Delta Delta
Founded: 1888
Colors: Silver, gold, and blue
Flower: Pansy
Web site: www.tridelta.org

ΔΓ

Delta Gamma
Founded: 1873
Colors: Bronze, pink, and blue
Flower: Cream-colored rose
Web site: www.deltagamma.org

ΔΦΕ

Delta Phi Epsilon
Founded: 1917
Colors: Royal purple and pure gold
Flower: Purple iris
Web site: www.dphie.org

ΔΖ

Delta Zeta
Founded: 1902
Colors: Rose and green
Flower: Pink Killarney rose
Web site: www.deltazeta.org

ΓΦΒ

Gamma Phi Beta
Founded: 1874
Colors: Pink and white
Flower: Pink carnation
Web site: www.gammaphibeta.org

ΚΑΘ

Kappa Alpha Theta
Founded: 1870
Colors: Black and gold
Flower: Black and gold pansy
Web site: www.kappaalphatheta.org

ΚΔ

Kappa Delta
Founded: 1897
Colors: Olive green and pearl white
Flower: White rose
Web site: www.kappadelta.org

ΚΚΓ

Kappa Kappa Gamma
Founded: 1870
Colors: Light blue and dark blue
Flower: Fleur-di-lis
Web site: www.kappakappagamma.org

ΦΜ

Phi Mu
Founded: 1852
Colors: Rose and white
Flower: Rose color carnation
Web site: www.phimu.org

ΦΣΣ

Phi Sigma Sigma
Founded: 1913
Colors: King blue and gold
Flower: American beauty rose
Web site: www.phisigmasigma.org

ΠΒΦ

Pi Beta Phi
Founded: 1867
Colors: Wine and silver blue
Flower: Wine carnation
Web site: www.pibetaphi.org

ΣΔΤ

Sigma Delta Tau
Founded: 1917
Colors: Café au lait and old blue
Flower: Golden tea rose
Web site: www.sigmadeltatau.com

ΣΚ

Sigma Kappa
Founded: 1874
Colors: Lavender and maroon
Flower: Violet
Web site: www.sigmakappa.org

ΣΣΣ

Sigma Sigma Sigma
Founded: 1898
Colors: Royal purple and white
Flower: Purple violet
Web site: www.sigmasigmasigma.org

ΘΦΑ

Theta Phi Alpha
Founded: 1912
Colors: Silver, gold, and blue
Flower: White rose
Web site: www.thetaphialpha.org

ΖΤΑ

Zeta Tau Alpha
Founded: 1898
Colors: Turquoise blue and steel gray
Flower: White violet
Web site: www.zetataualpha.org

Sororities that reflect the heritage, faith, or professions of their members

The National Pan-Hellenic Council

Founded in 1930 on the campus of Howard University, a historically black university, the organization includes four international Greek-letter sororities and five fraternities. The sororities are Alpha Kappa Alpha, Delta Sigma Theta, Zeta Phi Beta, and Sigma Gamma Rho.

Alpha Kappa Alpha, Delta Sigma Theta and Zeta Phi Beta Sororities all are charter member organizations of the National Pan-Hellenic Council. Sigma Gamma Rho Sorority joined in 1937. Alpha Kappa Alpha, which was founded at Howard in 1908, is the nation's first Greek-letter society for women.

Member Organizations of the National Pan-Hellenic Council

ΑΚΑ **Alpha Kappa Alpha**
Founded: 1908
Colors: Salmon pink and apple green
Flower: Pink tea rose
Web site: www.aka1908.com

ΔΣΘ **Delta Sigma Theta**
Founded: 1913
Colors: Crimson and cream
Flower: African violet
www.deltasigmatheta.org

ΖΦΒ **Zeta Phi Beta**
Founded: 1920
Colors: Blue and white
Flower: White rose
Web site: www.zphib1920.org

ΣΓΡ **Sigma Gamma Rho**
Founded: 1922
Colors: Royal blue and gold
Flower: Yellow tea rose
Web site: www.sgrho1922.org

Latina Sororities

The National Association of Latino Fraternal Organizations (NALFO), established in 1998, is an umbrella council for Latino Greek Letter Organizations. There are twenty-four member organizations from across the United States. Its Web site is www.nalfo.org.

The member organizations of the NALFO are:

ΑΠΣ

Alpha Pi Sigma
Founded: 1990 at San Diego State University
Colors: Pink and purple
Flower: Calla lily
Web site: www.alphapisigma.org

ΑΡΛ

Alpha Rho Lambda
Founded: 1993 at Yale University
Colors: Green and gold
Flower: Pink rose
Web site: www.alpharholambda.org

ΧΥΣ

Chi Upsilon Sigma
Founded: 1980 at the New Brunswick Campus of
  Rutgers
Colors: Red, black, and beige
Flower: Hibiscus
Web site: www.justbecus.org

ΓΑΩ

Gamma Alpha Omega
Founded: 1993
Colors: Navy blue, forest green, and white
Flower: White thornless rose
Web site: www.gammaalphaomega.com

ΓΦΩ

Gamma Phi Omega
Founded: 1991 at Indiana University, Bloomington
Primary Colors: Maroon and navy blue
Secondary Colors: Teal and gold
Flower: Fire and Ice rose
Web site: www.gammaphiomega.org

ΣΙΑ
Hermandad de Sigma Iota Alpha
Founded: 1990 at SUNY Albany, SUNY Stony Brook,
   SUNY New Paltz, and Rensselaer Polytechnic
   Institute
Colors: Red, gold, royal blue with black and white as
   background
Flower: Red rose
www.hermandad-sia.org

ΚΔΧ
Kappa Delta Chi
Founded: 1987
Colors: Pink and maroon
Flower: Pink rose
Web site: www.kappadeltachi.org

ΛΠΧ
Lambda Pi Chi
Founded: 1988 at Cornell University
Colors: Red, gold, black, and white
Flower: Red carnation
Web site: www.lambdapichi.org

ΛΘΑ
Lambda Theta Alpha
Founded: 1975 at Kean University in New Jersey
Colors: Burgundy and grey
Flower: Palm tree
Mascot: Penguin
Web site: www.lambdalady.org

ΛΘΝ
Lambda Theta Nu
Founded: March 11, 1986 at California State University,
   Chico
Colors: Silver, burgundy, and white
Flower: Rose
Web site: www.lambdathetanu.org

ΛΠΥ
Lambda Pi Upsilon
Founded: 1992 at State University of New York College
   at Geneseo
Colors: Red, white, gold, black
Flower: White rose with red tips
Web site: www.lpiu.com

ΘΦΒ
Omega Phi Beta Sorority
Founded: 1989 the University at Albany, State
   University of New York
Colors: Black, forest green, and gold
Flower: Sunflower
Web site: www.omegaphibeta.org

ΣΛΓ **Sigma Lambda Gamma**
Founded: 1990 at the University of Iowa
Colors: Shocking pink and majestic purple
Flower: Pink rose
Web site: www.sigmalambdagamma.com

ΣΛΥ **Sigma Lambda Upsilon**
Founded: 1987 at Binghamton University
Colors: Gold, black, silver, and red
Flower: Red pansy with gold and black
Web site: www.sigmalambdaupsilon.org

Asian American Sororities

Several Greek-letter organizations for women exist on specific campuses. Some of these sororities are located just on the campus where they were started, while others have expanded to other schools. They include:

ΧΑΔ **Chi Alpha Delta**
Founded: 1928 at the University of California, Los Angeles
Web site: www.chialphadelta.com

ΧΔΘ **Chi Delta Theta**
Founded: 1989 at University of California, Santa Barbara
Web site: www.chideltatheta.org

ΧΣΦ **Chi Sigma Phi**
Founded: 2000 at California State University, Fullerton
Colors: Lavender and white
Flower: Stargazer lily
Web site: www.geocities.com/chisigmaph

ΚΦΛ **Kappa Phi Lambda**
Founded: 1995 at Binghamton University
Colors: Scarlet red, white, heather grey
Flower: Orchid
Web site: www.kappaphilambda.org

ΣΦΩ **Sigma Phi Omega**
Founded: 1949 at the University of Southern California
Colors: Kelly green and maize yellow
Flower: Yellow rose
www.sigmaphiomega.com

Theta Kappa Phi
Founded: 1959 at University of California Los Angeles
Web site: www.thetakappaphi.com

Multicultural Sororities

Several Greek organizations for women were founded with the purpose of celebrating the varied heritage of its members. These groups prize the diversity of all members. Some are located only at the campus where they began, but many have expanded to other schools as well. Visit their Web sites for expansion plans and opportunities.

Multicultural sororities include:

Chi Sigma Upsilon Sorority, Inc.
Founded: 1993 at New Jersey City University
Colors: Burgundy and hunter green
Flower: Beavertail cactus
Web site: www.angelfire.com/nj/csu93/s

Chi Sigma Phi
Delta Xi Phi
Founded: 1994 on the University of Illinois at Urbana-Champaign
Colors: Navy blue and maroon
Flower: Yellow rose of Texas
Web site: www.geocities.com/~deltaxiphi

Iota Psi Phi
Founded: 1995 at California State University, Fresno
Colors: Black, brown, and white
Flower: White lily
Web site: www.csufresno.edu/StudentOrgs/IOTAPSIPHI

Lambda Psi Delta
Founded: 1997 at Yale University
Colors: Coal black and lily white
Flower: White calla lily
Web site: www.lambdapsidelta.org

Lambda Tau Omega
Founded: 1988 at Montclair State University
Colors: Royal blue and light gray
Web site: www.geocities.com/CollegePark/Lab/8874

ΩΦΧ **Omega Phi Chi**
Founded: 1988 at Rutgers University
Colors: Pink and black
Flower: Pink Lady slipper
Web site: www.omegaphichi.org

Religious and professional organizations

Some Greek-letter organizations reflect the faith, chosen professions, and academic excellence of their members. In some cases these are co-ed. Membership in a professional or academic honor society does not usually preclude membership in a traditional sorority as well.

Religious sororities include:

ΑΛΩ **Alpha Lambda Omega**
Founded: 1990 at University of Texas
Web site: studentorgs.utexas.edu/utalo/homepage.htm

ΣΑΩ **Sigma Alpha Omega**
Founded: 1998 at North Carolina State University
Web site: www.sigmaalphaomega.org

ΑΕΩ **Alpha Epsilon Omega**
Web site: www.alphaepsilonomega.net

ΛΟΧ **Lambda Omicron Chi**
Founded: 2002 at Old Dominion University
Colors: Azure blue and white
Web site: www.angelfire.com/va3/lox

ΣΦΛ **Sigma Phi Lambda**
Founded: 1988 at the University of Texas
Colors: Red and white
Web site: www.sigma-phi-lambda.com

ΣΑΕΠ **Sigma Alpha Epsilon Pi**
Founded: 1998 at University of California, Davis
Colors: Blue and gold
Flower: Blue iris
Web site: www.sigmaaepi.com

Professional sororities and honor societies

The Professional Fraternity Association, formed in 1978, is the umbrella organization overseeing career-oriented fraternities and sororities. Many of the organizations are co-ed. Its Web site is www. profraternity.org.

Professional Greek-letter organizations include:

ΑΧΣ
Alpha Chi Sigma
Career: Chemistry
Founded: 1902 at the University of Wisconsin
Web site: www.alphachisigma.org

ΚΕ
Kappa Epsilon
Career: Pharmacy
Founded: 1921 in Iowa
Web site: www.kappaepsilon.org

ΦΒ
Phi Beta
Career: Performing Arts
Founded: 1912 at Northwestern University
Web site: www.phibeta.com

ΣΑ
Sigma Alpha
Career: Agriculture
Founded: 1978 at Ohio State University
Colors: Emerald and maize
Flower: Yellow chrysanthemum
Web site: www.sigmaalpha.org

ΜΦΕ
Mu Phi Epsilon
Career: Music
Founded: 1903 at the Metropolitan College of Music in Cincinnati
Web site: muphiepsilon.org

ΦΔΕ
Phi Delta Epsilon
Career: Medicine
Founded: 1904 at Cornell University Medical College
Web site: www.phide.org

ΣΦΔ
Sigma Phi Delta
Career: Engineering
Founded: 1924 at the University of Southern California
Web site: www.sigmaphidelta.org

ΠΣΕ **Pi Sigma Epsilon**
Career: Marketing
Founded: 1952 at Georgia State University
Web site: www.pse.org

ΦΧΘ **Phi Chi Theta**
Career: Business and economics
Founded: 1924 in Chicago
Web site: www.phichitheta.org

Honor organizations include Phi Beta Kappa, the country's first and largest academic honor society.

ΦΒΚ **Phi Beta Kappa**
Founded: 1776 at the College of William & Mary
Web site: www.pbk.org

Starting a new chapter

You might think recruitment was a long and involved process, but it's nothing compared to the process of extension, when a new chapter of a sorority is started at a college.

Much like recruitment, this process involves mutual selection. The sorority will evaluate whether a certain campus is a good prospect for a chapter, and the college will consider which sorority will be a good addition to its Greek system.

The process generally begins when a college or university votes to extend its Greek system. It will let the member organizations of the National Panhellenic Conference know that extension opportunities exist. Each sorority that does not already have a chapter there will decide whether to pursue extension at that school.

When considering campuses for extension of new chapters, a sorority will look at several factors, including:

- The strength and growth of the Greek system at that school, and whether there has ever been a chapter of that sorority there.

- The number of sorority alumnae in the area.

- The strength and ranking of the university in question.

- The time and financial commitments involved—whether the sorority would need to purchase or build a house or could move into an existing one, etc.

- The support on campus of the Greek system.

Once a sorority has decided that a school would be a good prospect for extension, members from its national headquarters will provide informational materials to the school. Representatives from several sororities may be invited to give presentations at the college. The college will then decide which sorority or sororities will be invited to colonize (form a new chapter of the sorority).

The colonization process will begin with an awareness campaign to let students know that the XY sorority is coming to campus. There may be formal or informal parties, and representatives from the sorority will come to campus to meet potential new members. The process of selecting new members is a streamlined recruitment. Instead of an entire house full of members making the selections, the decisions are left up to the sorority's representatives on campus.

A bid day celebration is held to welcome the new members. A colonization ceremony follows to officially establish the sorority at its new campus.

The new colony's members will go through a period of learning about their sorority's history, bylaws, and traditions. It is similar to the pledge process at an established chapter. Representatives of the sorority, which may include a residential consultant, will guide the girls through this process, as there are no current members.

At the conclusion of this process, the new colony's members are officially initiated into the sorority. The sorority's national president and other high-ranking representatives often attend this ceremony, which is known as installation.

Now the new colony has become an official chapter, and the newest girls have become official members. It's one of the most exciting times for a sorority, but it does not happen often or quickly. If you are interested in forming a new chapter of a sorority that is not on your campus, contact your school's Panhellenic office for guidance.

CHAPTER FIFTEEN

Star Power:

Celebrity Sorority Alums

Star Power:
Celebrity Sorority Alums

Almost everywhere you look, you'll find high-achieving women whose college life included sorority membership. Chapters are naturally proud to claim their notable alumnae, often listing them among other information.

Here are some of the most well-known former sorority women making great strides in all facets of society. You'll find notable Greek alumnae

...on the big and small screens:

Joy Behar	Lucy Liu
Julia Louis-Dreyfus	Meg Ryan
Jennifer Garner	Jada Pinkett Smith
Goldie Hawn	Sela Ward
Patricia Heaton	Vanessa Williams
Ashley Judd	

....in political life:

Madeleine Albright	Lynne Cheney
Barbara Bush	Elizabeth Dole
Jenna Bush	Tipper Gore
Laura Bush	Condoleeza Rice

...on the United States Supreme Court:

Ruth Bader Ginsburg

...on the pop, country, and Christian music charts:

Deana Carter
Sheryl Crow

Amy Grant
Jewel

....they're in the fashion world:

Christie Brinkley
Liz Claiborne
Cindy Crawford

Kathy Ireland
Betsey Johnson
Kate Spade

...or out of this world (astronauts):

Jan Davis
Sally Ride

Rhea Seddon
Mary Ellen Weber

...you've seen them on television:

Katie Couric
Catherine Crier
Leeza Gibbons
Kathie Lee Gifford

Star Jones
Deborah Norville
Jane Pauley

...or read their books:

Maya Angelou
Sue Grafton

Harper Lee
Billie Letts

...and some are in a class all to themselves:

The late Rosa Parks, civil rights legend

Famous fraternity men:
Will you meet a future politician, artist, writer, or actor at a mixer?

The list of fraternity celebs includes:

George H. W. Bush

George W. Bush

Drew Carey

Johnny Carson

Kenny Chesney

Bill Cosby

Kevin Costner

Will Ferrell

Harrison Ford

Theodor Geisel (Dr. Seuss)

Woody Harrelson

Michael Jordan

John F. Kennedy Jr.

Martin Luther King, Jr.

Ashton Kutcher

Nick Lachey

David Letterman

Matthew McConaghey

Tim McGraw

Paul Newman

Brad Pitt

Robert Redford

Fred Savage

David Schwimmer

Tavis Smiley

David Spade

Steven Spielberg

Jerry Springer

Jon Stewart

Ted Turner

Blair Underwood

Keenan Wayans

Acknowledgements

We hope you find *Sorority Guide* useful during the recruitment process and afterward. Sorority membership can be a rewarding experience, and we're honored to be a small part of your journey. Before, during, and after your recruitment process, we hope you'll visit us on-line at www.sororityguide.com. You'll find more great tips and resources, along with a forum to share your recruitment experiences.

We want to thank all the incredible women who helped in the creation of *Sorority Guide*. Gina Pia Bandini, founder and editor of FashionFinds.com, is an expert on teen style and fashion. She and Sharon Haver, founder and style director of FocusOnStyle.com, shared fabulous fashion tips. Stress-management expert Donna Brooks gave us awesome tools to help you keep your cool.

Dr. Jean Twenge, assistant professor at San Diego State University's Department of Psychology, Dr. Mark R. Leary, professor and chair in the Department of Psychology at Wake Forest University, and Dr. Lyndon Waugh, a clinical psychiatrist and author, shared important insights on handling the stress of recruitment while keeping everything in perspective.

Journalist and communications consultant Margot Carmichael Lester taught us to look great in ink, while Tena Roberts and Jeff Rankin shared their knowledge of sorority history. We found lots of terrific tips and fun facts from hundreds of collegiate and Greek Web sites.

We owe a big thank-you to all the current and alumnae sorority members who told us their hilarious memories and a few horror stories. Their experiences hold invaluable lessons for all prospective new sorority members. We enjoyed meeting with each one.

Thanks to our family and friends for their support and suggestions.

To our own sorority sisters, a special thank you. We cherish the memories of rushing and pledging, of learning songs to sing and skits to perform for the rushees who came after us. We'll never forget the fun we shared at pledge swaps and formals, working on charitable projects, and just spending time together, really becoming sisters. Thanks, ladies, for the roles you have played throughout our lives.

To every girl in search of a Greek home, good luck!

All the best, C.H. and A.S.

BOTTOM LINE:

To talk about this book, get help, or check out other cool sorority ideas, go to www.sororityguide.com today!

Index

About the Authors

Ceil Howle and Anna Stephens, award-winning business executives with an international cosmetics corporation and a Fortune 500 corporation, recognized the need to help girls level the playing field in the competitive arena of Greek life. Their life experiences from the professional world, community involvement, and raising teenagers and their successful personal experiences with sororities inspired them to share these success strategies and expert advice.

Jennifer Brett is a feature writer for a major metropolitan newspaper who specializes in the personal aspect of teen topics. She has covered everything from *American Idol* contestants to sensational front-page headlines.